They Said, "Teach Us More"

Solos, Winter Hiking & Overnighters

Kenneth Bosse

Copyright © 2023   Kenneth J. Bosse
ISBN: 978-1-7343315-3-0
All rights reserved.

The characters and events portrayed in this book are semi-fictitious. Any similarity to real persons (apart from those personally known to the author) living or dead, is coincidental and not intended by the author.

No part of this book may be reproduced, or stored in a retrieval system, or transmitted in any form or by any means, electronic, mechanical, photocopying, recording, or otherwise, without express written permission of the publisher.

Cover design by: Kenneth Bosse

About the Cover

Pictured on the cover are a crew of NH Fish & Game officers who oversee search and rescue in the state. The other picture is the Pemigewasset Search and Rescue team. I had the privilege of hiking with both these teams in extreme winter conditions when most people stay home, sit by the fire, and drink hot chocolate. The stories are found in the pages of this book. Needless to say, these teams gleaned from my wisdom of backwoods ruggedness.

Most people don't know the true history of how search and rescue teams started so let me enlighten you.

Back in 1758, little Noah Dent Gitlost went walking in the woods with his dog Lightning. As they wandered farther into the deep woods of Berlin, NH, Lightning scented a rabbit and took off like . . . well, like lightning. Noah started running after him, calling, "Lightning, come. Lightning, come!" Seems like Noah did not notice the dark clouds that had formed on Mt. Cabot and out of those clouds, lightning came.

The bolt from the sky struck a bull pine and it came down, knocking Gitlost to the ground and pinning him there. Lightning (the dog) knew this was serious poo poo and took off for help.

When the townspeople saw Lightning was alone, they figured Noah must be lost. All the men gathered for the purpose of doing a search in order to rescue little Noah. (See what just happened there? Search AND rescue!)

After 18 long hours of searching, some men heard Lightning barking. Of course, Lightning tried to lead the men straight to Noah, but he had taken off like . . . really fast. The men eventually found Noah, freed him from the tree and, as they were hiking out, got the idea to fish a bit and hunt some game. (Again, fish AND game!). Truth is stranger than fiction.

Anyhow, weeks later, old farmer Kneeland said, "We should start a search and rescue team and call it Fish and Game." And so, it was unofficially born.

Little Noah would get teased in the following months about getting lost. In retaliation, he would scream his name over and over, "Noah Dent Gitlost!"

Well, there you have it. Now let's get into the riches of wisdom in this book.

TABLE OF CONTENTS

		Page
	Author's Note	i
	Cast of Characters	ii
	Introduction	iv
	Categories of Hikers	viii
	What's the Dope on Winter Hiking the Whites?	ix
1	Mount Pierce: Winter Hike	1
2	Cannon Mountain: Winter Hike	3
3	Mount Liberty: Solo Winter Hike	7
4	Mount Roberts: Winter Hike	11
5	The Pemigewasset Search & Rescue Team	13
6	It's Raining Cats & Dogs	23
7	First Overnighter	27
8	Second Overnighter	31
9	Third Overnighter: Total Fail	35
10	Training with NH Fish & Game: Mt. Cardigan Winter Hike	37
11	Jennings Peak & Sandwich Mountain: Winter Hike	45
12	Jennings Peak: Winter Hike	49
13	The Gunstock Loop: Winter Hike	53
14	Fourth Overnighter	57
15	Fifth Overnighter	61
16	The Hike of a Lifetime	67
17	Winter Solo Overnighter	69
18	Eveready Bunny vs. Roadkill	75
19	Tents	79
20	The Tale of Two Climates: Solo Hike	81
21	Hair of the Dog	85

22	Why Do You Hike?	87
23	Simple, Quick Overnighter	91
24	The Sandwich Dome Makeup Test	95
25	Osceola: Overnighter	99
26	Ducks, Deer, Bear & Solo Hiking	103
27	Kearsarge North: 4th of July Solo Hike	107
28	Mount Moosilauke: Solo	111
29	Trail Wisdom: Play It Safe When Solo Hiking	115
30	Liar, Liar, Pants on Fire	119
31	The Holt Trail: When You Have an Injury but Not Too Many Brains	121
32	Boy, You're Gonna Carry That Weight	125
33	Mount Paugus: Solo Hiking Ghosts	129
34	The Deer Fly: Overnighter	133
35	Old Age & Hiking	137
36	The Hiker Babes	141
37	When Hell Freezes Over	149
38	Last Overnighter of the Season	153
39	Conclusion	157
	About the Editor	159
	About the Author	161

Author's Note

The main focus of this book will include winter hiking, solo hiking and overnighters. There is no chronological order, just an assortment of stories that cover all three topics. I hope you laugh a lot and learn a little. I also hope you will get out there and try a hike for yourself. By definition, I am the worst hiker in New Hampshire, probably in the world. If I can do it, anyone can. So get out there and suffer a little, it's great fun.

WARNING: This book contains content that some may consider highly offensive. Years ago, this content was known as humor. If you get your knickers in a bunch, you have probably been butt-sliding down steep trails in the winter or you are overly sensitive. Learn to laugh a little, it's OK. Most of my humor comes from observing the moronic stuff I do — and my reflection in the bathroom mirror.

Cast of Characters

As with my first two books, the main cast changed little.

Keith is the oldest. He is also the calmest, especially when driving. It is everyone else in the vehicle that is having a panic attack, screaming in horror and fainting.

Dave is the PITA. That does not stand for People for the Ethical Treatment of Animals, but rather Pain In The A$$. For him, it is a life calling.

Caroline is married to Ian. When she goes with us, she is the buffer that causes these goons to somewhat behave.

Ian is the guy who never gets rattled. Unless there are ladders, caves, technical rock formations, chimneys, cliff walks, steep ice flows and ... well, you get the idea.

Darlene, my lovely wife, is faced with the challenge of maintaining my psych meds. Funny, I never needed them until I took up hiking with the goons.

Introduction

I really enjoy hiking. I love the solitude of the forests and the rejuvenation of being alone on ancient mountains. If they could talk, I would sit in silence and listen to their tales. I also love people. All people. I'm not prejudiced or phobic of anyone or anything. People, like mountains, have fascinating life stories to share. However, with the recent surge of people flocking to the mountains, there comes a strange mixture of the two and I am torn. My two joys are sometimes in conflict.

After hiking for many years, I have discovered there are numerous categories that most hikers fall into. This variety is what makes up the spice of the hiking community. Most people are the nicest you would ever want to meet. They are courteous and kind, willing to share and always ready to help.

Then there is me.

Categories of hikers

1) The athletes: These folks are ripped and have definable six-pack abs. They eat lettuce and kale and actually feel good about it. Most consume large quantities of powdered organic drink mix no one quite knows the contents of. They view hiking as a workout. Instead of going to the gym they consider running up the Flume Slide Trail as good fun. I am always intimidated when I encounter an athlete on the trail. I feel like they are judging my clumsy, overweight appearance. It may be in my mind, but then I hear them giggling as they trot off with their 60-pound packs filled with salad. These people lost their marbles somewhere in childhood. Come on, folks, you know when you eventually die at 126 years of age you are going to regret not enjoying that double cheeseburger. You are, however, pretty amazing, so rock on!

2) The sunny, weekend warriors: These are your family types who hike with three kids under 5 and the baby in the carry-on backpack, while being skirted by four family dogs named Kesha, Broady, Figgels and Squirts. The latter gets its name from digesting the other three dogs' pre-digested, and eliminated, Kibbles-n-Bites Meaty Middles. These eco-friendly types are the ones who scoop the poop, place it in little blue bags, then leave them along the sides of trails for the Poop Fairy to dispose of. I tip my hat in respect to the two moms of a small fraternity of young'uns I met as they were butt-sliding their way down Percy Peak (one of the steepest trails I've been on). I'm sure those kids will grow up with undaunted confidence or be traumatized for life. Seriously, I am delighted to see families do things together. Those memories last forever.

News flash: there is no Poop Fairy.

3) The young singles: You can spot them 200 feet off. They always hike solo, wear strong perfume or aftershave, show off their mid-sections, including tats, and rarely acknowledge anyone other than young solo hikers of the opposite sex. I mean, come on folks, there are websites for this kind of stuff. Who knows? Maybe that mountain magic will lead to a mountain marriage. As a minister, let me offer my services should love strike like a lightning bolt, causing you to want to get married on a mountain. For a moderate fee, I can officiate your wedding on the summit of your choice, as long as your choice is Mount Willard.

"It gives me great joy to introduce Mr. and Mrs. . . . ."

Just so the young singles can enjoy a line in this book exclusively for them ... "I am taking it offline, after growth-hacking the bio break."

4) The middle-aged women groups: Yup, they are always in groups. I have witnessed them in threes and in mobs of 30. In my younger dating experiences, I discovered that women cannot go to the bathroom alone, so it only goes to figure. I need to tread lightly as they make up one of the largest categories of hikers and, if they ever recognize me on a trail, I doubt I could hold my own against six of them coming at me with their hiking poles. My hope is, as with a bear attack, if I play dead, it will call forth their motherly, nurturing instincts and I will soon be pampered with trail snacks. I will say, this category is the most talkative. The fastest land wind speeds were recorded on Mount Washington when a group of 35 of them were talking about *The Bachelorette*. In fear of losing trail snacks, I'll stop there.

5) The child prodigies: Forget Paw Patrol and Dora the Explorer, these adorable little 5-year-old mountaineers get excited about knocking off the Winter 48 in 29 days. I have no words. I am sure, given enough time, that one of them will be the first to knock off every peak in Alaska and then make a Netflix documentary about it. What next? First baby to crawl Mount Washington?

We salute you.

6) The "What the heck is that?" This is the 60-year-old nerdy guy who carries enough 30-year-old gear to permanently live above treeline. He wears a bear bell the size of a tennis ball that gongs like a Tibetan monastery, while listening to *Technology Today* through his ear buds. He has a hat made of real Yaks fur and it's hard to tell where the Yak ends and he begins. You cannot miss this guy. He wears a down jacket that is so big he looks like a giant blue marshmallow, but it is offset by his shorts, white socks and sandals. His homemade hiking pole looks as if it doubles as a murder weapon that causes people to give him a wide berth while trampling over fragile mountain flora and fauna.

Oops, I think I just described one of the guys I hike with.

7) The non-hiker hikers: These well-meaning folks live in the world of "what if." They wear the latest North Face jacket and Patagonia pants. They carry a small Osprey butt pack filled with lip balm and credit cards. They're sporting Oakley shades and Loro Piana hiking boots while never setting foot on anything steeper than the walkway to the Mount Washington Hotel.

Dang, that was harsh.

8) The busload of college students: Encountering them is like watching the trailer to an end-of-the-world disaster movie. You just know someone's going to get hurt. Only a quarter of them are shouldering packs, none of the others seem to have any water or food. Usually you will see them close to the trailhead and never on the summits (which is probably a good thing); they are always laughing and having fun, wearing the latest designer sneakers and fashion jeans with the made-to-order tears in the fabric. The funny thing is on either side of the trail are the wannabe-young-again folks taking notes as if the trail is a fashion runway. "Oh, look at those sneakers. Are they Valentino's or Jimmy Choo's? Oh my! Are those jeans Diesel Safados?" I usually walk away shaking my head, saying, "That Gucci purse would make a great snack bag."

These student groups should really reconsider a trip to downtown Boston. Lots of history there and the terrain is flat.

9) The "Still Hiking At 85" folks: These individuals usually have worn, cracked, weathered skin with beard stubble. The men, on the other hand, have full beards and bright blue eyes that communicate smiles and sunshine. Their slow, yet steady, crawl reveals years of mountain experience. To these people, we respectfully approach with admiration and humbly ask if they would share a story, knowing their stories are filled with wisdom. To which they usually respond by saying, "Get the hell out of my way, you're wrecking my mojo!"

Yup.

10) The parent/adult-child hiking team: The bonding that takes place is real, folks. The parent can usually be heard complimenting and encouraging the adult-child who, in turn, is outpacing the parent with speed, grace, balance and technical rock scrambling skill, while muttering constantly under their breath. I remember seeing one such mother-daughter team that were not happy hikers. I thought for sure I would read about a mountain murder in the morning paper.

No bedtime stories for those trophy-winning darlings.

I know I started off by saying, "After hiking for years, you will discover that there are numerous categories..." Who am I kidding? With the rate of popularity at which hiking has exploded, you can run into all 10 categories on any given weekend.

Notice I didn't include a category for older out-of-shape men who struggle up every trail – because this is not an autobiography.

What's The Dope on Winter Hiking the Whites?

About one-third of this book will be given to discussing winter hiking, including some winter hikes I have just recently finished. People have so many questions and rightfully so. Where do I begin?

Let us start with the definition of terms such as the alpine zone, layering, traction, monorail, spruce traps, bonked, gram weenies, stupid light, hypothermia and imminent death, to name a few.

The alpine zone: This refers to the area of a mountain that extends above treeline. It is directly connected with **hypothermia** and **imminent death**, but I will come back to those. Cold, windy and adverse conditions do not allow most plants to survive above treeline. Yet some that do are extremely fragile and vulnerable to human traffic. They usually do not survive being repeatedly trampled on. Please use every effort to stay on marked trails. If you do not comply, the plants will send out a signal that makes its way into your salad and you will experience explosive diarrhea accompanied by the inability to stop sneezing.

Harsh conditions leave much of the alpine zones bare rock, so trails are marked by cairns. Cairns are stacked rockpiles, usually 2 to 4 feet high. In winter conditions, these markers are the only way to find trails, preventing you from wandering off a 200-foot cliff. If you playfully build your own rock stacks, you may inadvertently send someone else off a 200-foot drop. Building stacks of rocks in the presence of winter hikers can lead to what some refer to as a butt-kicking.

Being above treeline in the alpine zone is a wonderful experience. It has a beauty all its own. Being above treeline in the winter is another matter. Here is where people die. It is not uncommon in the White Mountains to have windchills down to -60° F. You must be prepared, and you must give great attention to weather forecasts. Hypothermia leads to mental fog that results in bad decisions that can lead to imminent death. Please do not come to New Hampshire just to die. Do that in your own state. I once summited Mount Jackson at -30° F. Needless to say, it was unpleasant.

Layering: In my world, layering has two meanings. The first is when Dave, Ian and Keith start busting on me, not allowing the antics (which I participate in) to be evenly dispersed. This layering starts getting old after a week of abuse, usually leading to another term called **solo hiking**. The second meaning refers to winter apparel. Layering refers to the proper way of dressing for winter hiking. You do not want to wear your big, heavy winter jacket you use at home. When you hike, you sweat. When you sweat, you soak clothing. When you soak clothing, you get cold. When you get sweaty and cold, you die. Most of the time, layering is referencing three main layers. The first, called a base layer, is usually made of a self-wicking material that absorbs sweat, causing it to dry quickly. The second layer is called a mid-layer consisting of a heavier thermal barrier such as polyester fleece, Merino wool or goose down. If you are a heavy sweater like I am, the outer layer and mid-layer may need to be removed before you start sweating, so you will want room in your pack to stow them away. Also, you will want layers that are compressible to stow easily. The outer layer needs to be a wind-blocking shell or rain layer. Part of the fun of winter hiking is the need to stop every tenth of a mile to layer or delayer as needed. If you are fortunate, after a while, you will discover that sweet spot somewhere between freezing your buns off and roasting like a pig on the spit. I will also point out that as you start buying layers, you are experimenting and seeking that perfect combination, leading to four closets full of assorted layers.

Happy layering.

Traction: Again, referring to the incessant needling of Dave, Ian and Keith, traction in a hospital is where they will end up if they do not alter their ways. I digress. Traction refers to what you need to wear on your feet in various winter conditions. **Bare booting** refers to hiking with just hiking boots or winter boots — it does not include clogs or sneakers. As snow and ice make their appearance, you need to wear spikes. Not the junk you get at the Cheap O Depots, but good, quality spikes such as Hillsound, Cimkiz or Kahtoola. Spikes are lifesavers and allow you to walk right up an ice flow without fear. If you are mountaineering up steep stuff you will want to trade in your spikes for crampons. Crampons have larger, longer spikes with some toe prongs that allow you to dig into the side of a steep incline. Wearing spikes does not mean you will not fall. When you get tired and your legs turn to mush, you stand the chance of catching a spike from one foot into the pants of the other leg. Trust me, those are the best wipeouts you will ever have. Last are snowshoes. When Old Man Winter decides to take a dump on New Hampshire, we can get clobbered by a good old-fashioned Nor'easter. I was 19 when we were hit with "Storm Larry." This Blizzard of 1978 started on Feb. 5 and didn't let up until Feb. 7. It deposited almost 28 inches of wet, heavy snow that cost the lives of 100 people and cost in today's market $2.6 billion in damages. The dollar amount does not reflect the $3 million for snowshoes that everyone went out and bought, wore three times, then placed in yard sales.

I have a love/hate relationship with snowshoes. I love to hate them. They are a workout times 10. If you are going to hike in winter, it is inevitable that you will need snowshoes. It is not uncommon to start a hike with spikes and find that higher up there are 3-foot drifts on the trails. Another term associated with winter hiking is **breaking trail.** This means you are the first slob to hit a trail after snowfall and you are the lucky winner to pack it all down for the pleasure of folks like me. Breaking trail is excruciating work and many times leads to breaking wind that can lend itself to breaking friendships, which you do not want to do, because breaking trail is best done in teams. Like geese flying south, the one in the front gets plum worn out and falls back so another can take the lead. When I am on such a team, I always find reasons to fall behind. Layering, hydration, snack break, bathroom break ... This ensures I will never be in front. Did it once, ended up in traction (not the footwear).

I was in my teens when I was first traumatized by the old, wooden, Michigan-style snowshoes. They weighed as much as a couple of cinder blocks. They had the uncanny ability to sink 12 inches in only 8 inches of snow, allowing five pounds of snow to fall on them and causing the up-step action to be excruciating. Their width would result in overlapping when you stopped so that when you resumed you would immediately do a face plant. With the ignorance of youth, I thought I was having fun.

I just purchased my third pair of snowshoes because I am always looking for a pair that will somehow make snowshoeing easy. My new pair are MSR *Lightning Ascent* snowshoes. There is nothing in that name that even remotely represents my snowshoeing pace. My old shoes were Tubbs — that name is more like it. I've lost count of all the times I have lashed my snowshoes onto my pack only to take them for a six-mile walk. You have to do it or run the risk of the dreaded posthole when you ruin the sacred ...

Monorails: These are the holy grail of winter hiking. Monorails are the compressed, hard-packed surface that the snowshoers have suffered through to make trails easy for bums like me to hike on with just spikes. However, when the snow softens you can break through the hardened bridge and sink up to your knees, leaving the monorail looking like Swiss cheese. If a dyed-in-the-wool snowshoer witnesses such an act, you best hope you can make a lightning ascent — and I am not talking about the snowshoes.

Spruce traps: Between summits in the **alpine zone** are areas that can accumulate large quantities of deep snow. Below the snow are small shrubs of spruce that are stunted by the brutal winter conditions. When a hiker gets off trail and wanders into these areas, they discover the wonder referred to as the **spruce trap**. This is how it plays out: the hiker is in trouble and getting concerned about being off trail as the winds are rising and the temps are dropping. He decides to bail. That is a term meaning to go down as fast as you can. He is already tired and starting to shiver. He crosses a col between peaks and finds himself sinking up to his waist in snow. What he does not know is that below the snow are spruce bushes that act like curled bear teeth pointing downward. While the stepping into was nothing, the stepping out of becomes nearly impossible. Fleeing the changing weather, he trudges on. Each pulling out of a spruce trap saps his energy at hypersonic speeds while he tries to escape the jaws of hell. The next thing he knows he is …

Bonked: I am not making this up. **Bonking** is a term used to describe the sudden fatigue caused by the loss of energy due to the depletion of carbohydrates. It is also referred to in other athletic activities as "hitting the wall." This is what happens: first you feel an incredible amount of energy as if a long-desired superpower has manifested. You can do anything! Soon after, the car runs out of gas and you find yourself weak, tired, sweating, feeling dizzy or lightheaded, and you may have heart palpitations or see visions of your friends actually caring for you. In one article I read, the author said he can remember bonking three times in his life. After hiking hundreds of mountains, I can remember three hikes I did not bonk on. For me it is a vicious cycle of trying to lose weight and continuing hiking. I get BONKED every time. Darlene thought I was caring on with an affair when using these fangled hiking terms. No, but in some way, there is an overlapping definition of terms. The best way to avoid bonking is celibacy. Ha, sorry. I couldn't resist. Seriously, you need to eat a high-caloric breakfast, and, on the trail, you need to have high-calorie snacks every hour to ensure the tank stays full. Some popular snacks are Shot Blocks or Stingers. Good old-fashioned candy bars also work well.

Gram weenie: Dear God, where do people come up with this stuff? OK, let's face it: no one likes lugging around unnecessary weight. You do not need that frying pan to hike Cannon Mountain. Just bring a sandwich. You do not need a trauma medical kit, just the basics. There comes a time when you have to question the sanity of weight control. As a novice you start off with the mentality of "What's a few extra pounds?" You soon realize after a 16-mile traverse that those pounds add up. OK, time to cut back. Then there comes a shift when you start counting ounces. I am a big fan of the new ultralight hiking gear. They remove extra weight while removing your life's savings. There are, however, some in the hiking community that start counting grams, thus **gram weenies**. I do not know who came up with the name and don't care. But it is rather funny. What can we count next? Milligrams? Micrograms? For me, even counting ounces is a little over the top when I stop to realize I am physically 25 to 30 pounds overweight.

To cut those pounds means cutting carbs and now we are back to getting bonked. The struggle is real, folks. For the person who achieves nirvana with their pack weight comes the next term ...

Stupid-light: These people no longer hike, they levitate. They have removed so much weight they hike the Northern Presidential Traverse with nothing but shorts. Not even shoes, just shorts. Sure, they end up in the hospital or needing a rescue, but at least they are light to carry out. **Stupid-light**.

Hypothermia: I have talked extensively about this in my first two books. Suffice it to say during winter hiking is when it usually hits and "it" entails freezing you rear-end off. In extreme cases people have removed all their gear and even stripped clothing off as their minds became confused. Either that or they wanted to become **stupid-light**. As I write this story, tomorrow's mountain forecast is calling for -44° F. That is beyond my comfort zone by about 54°. When it is too cold out, stay home.

So let's put all the pieces together. You are above treeline in the **alpine zone**, you do not have the proper **layering**, you left your **traction** in the car because you are a **gram weenie** who is now **stupid-light**. You have gotten off the **monorail**, getting stuck in **spruce traps**, you just got **bonked** and now suffer from **hypothermia**. You have now arrived at the final destination of ... **imminent death**.

There, doesn't that make you feel better about winter hiking in the Whites?

1 MOUNT PIERCE
Winter Hike

Although only Dec. 20 and just 24 hours from the official start to winter, I am counting this one as my first winter hike of 2021. The weather and trail conditions did not change one iota. Both days started out cold, around 5° F, with the same weather and trail conditions. So just pretend it is Dec. 21, and everything will work out fine.

Ian had promised Caroline and I a casual, go-at-your-own pace hike up Mt. Pierce. We stopped for a pit stop at the AMC Highland Center at Crawford Notch and, upon exiting the car, experienced our first shock of the chilly northern air. That is the moment you reevaluate winter hiking.

After arriving at the trailhead parking lot, Caroline decided to layer up. I started moseying my way up the trail, drinking in every sensation of the frosty morning in the woods. When they caught up to me, Caroline was ready to shed some of the just-added layers. The trail was well-packed, allowing us to hike with just spikes for traction. The snowshoes on my pack would stay there. The sky was a deep-blue and the evergreens were frosted over. It was a glorious morning.

At 4,313 feet, Mount Pierce is the smallest in the Presidential Range. Formerly called Mount Clinton for the 19th-century Gov. DeWitt Clinton of New York, it was renamed after President Franklin Pierce, who happens to be the only president born in New Hampshire. Although the range begins with Mount Webster and Mount Jackson, the latter is not named after a president but rather a geologist. The trail follows the Crawford Path, the oldest continually used hiking trail in the United States.

What made this hike hilarious was Caroline and I were not in sync. She would stop to hydrate, 10 minutes later I would stop to delayer, another 10 minutes later she would stop to delayer, a while later I would stop to hydrate, then she stopped for a snack, I followed with my own snack 10 minutes later. Mister "Hike as Slow as You Want" was losing his mind. He actually started griping and complaining by the time we summited. It was hysterical. He started whining about being deprived of scooting over to Mount Eisenhower. He had a pout on that would shame any three-year-old. He even recorded our stop/start pattern by showing us the Strava graph of the hike. An EKG of the lad would have revealed the same pattern. There is a trail acronym called HYOH. It stands for "Hike Your Own Hike." So much for HYOH.

As Ian cooled down, the temps warmed up and even though the 1.2-mile trek over to Eisenhower would have been nice, we decided to head out.

The summit vista in every direction was picturesque. Snowcapped peaks were declaring the majesty of why the Whites are called the Whites. We made good time heading down and, though uneventful, just the joy of being in the woods with friends was rewarding enough.

The lesson I gleaned from this hike was that every hike is different. I've hiked Pierce at least five or six times and each one was unique. I believe that is why people keep returning to the mountains. Every season, every weather condition, every change in your circumstances or attitude makes the same changeless mountain a new experience. It is part of the mystique that calls us back.

Winter seems to heighten your senses to the surroundings. The crunching of the snow under your feet, the sting of the cool air on your cheeks, breath turned to steam — it all creates winter magic. The bright winter sunlight reflecting off the pure white snow, the deep green spruce frosted in white, streams turned to ice, blowdowns and twisted hardwoods are all beautiful in the winter. The forests seem thinner with foliage removed and shrubs buried. It may seem barren, but it sure makes you feel alive. Add to all that Ian's irritation and you have the perfect winter hike.

2 Cannon Mountain
Winter Hike

Cannon Mountain is a 4,083-foot peak in the White Mountains of New Hampshire. It is known for both its technical rock and ice climbing on its cliff face, and skiing at Cannon Mountain Ski Area. It was also home to the Old Man of the Mountain, a rock formation giving the appearance of a man's profile.

The image became synonymous with the state. Daniel Webster famously said, "Men hand out their signs indicative of their respective trades; shoemakers hand out a gigantic shoe; jewelers a monster watch, and the dentist hangs out a gold tooth; but up in the Mountains of New Hampshire God Almighty has hung out a sign to show that there He makes men." As a native of New Hampshire, I enjoyed visiting the Old Man for years until the formation collapsed on May 3, 2003.

Cannon Cliff is the largest vertical rock face in the Northeast. It is roughly 1,000 feet high and more than one mile long, according to a Summit-Post description, "Some of the aid lines are long and difficult enough to require a bivy, making Cannon the only Big Wall in the Northeast." Cannon is popular with free- and aid-climbers in summer and ice and mixed climbers in winter. Several rock and ice guidebooks exist for Cannon and Franconia Notch, most notably "Secrets of the Notch" by Jon Sykes. (Wikipedia)

Most people do not know that on April 2, 1973, the second strongest surface wind gust ever recorded in the United States was measured by University of Massachusetts researchers on the summit of Cannon. Although wind velocity was measured at 199.5 mph, this reading represents the physical limit of the recording instrument, and thus the true value may have been quite higher. Only the record value measured on nearby Mount Washington in 1934 exceeds this. (Wikipedia)

Also, Abigale French, who in 1921, while bellowing out 592 words a minute hit gusts of 215 mph. (Ken-apedia) If there is an Abigale French out there, I claim artistic license.

Cannon got its name on my first hike up. While on the summit, I flexed my biceps and someone below shouted, "Look at those cannons."

Give me some butter, I'm on a roll. Ha!

OK, I'll stop.

Seriously, Cannon is named after a rock formation on the southeast side of the mountain that looks like a cannon. Cannon has three sub-peaks known as The Cannon Balls. Hiking Cannon is a blast. Just don't have a short fuse. (Sorry.)

On Dec. 24, 2021, Ian, Caroline and I headed up for what would be my third hike up Cannon. Previously I had hiked up with Ian and Keith by way of the Lonesome Lake Trail, then we took the south approach of the Kinsman Ridge Trail to the summit. One of those hikes encompassed two seasons. Fall, at the lower elevations, and an Antarctic winter at the top. Keith and Ian complained quite a bit, but it was still a good hike overall. With Ian and Caroline, we took the north side of the Kinsman Ridge Trail, which is insanely steep. Once again, we started off at 5° F with a slight overcast, but the temps rose into the 20's. The lovebirds used snowshoes, while I went with spikes. It is always a 50-50 call on what to wear. They did better on moderate grades, I did better on the steep stuff. It was all steep. Holy smokes, what a pull. We found ourselves stopping often to recover. To the north, we saw an undercast entering Franconia Notch and crashing into Franconia Ridge to the east. It was amazing.

Two-thirds of the way up, there is an epic overview facing Franconia Ridge. It is the perfect spot for glamour shots with Mounts Liberty, Lincoln and Lafayette in the background.

What happened next was straight from The Twilight Zone. I will relay the facts accurately and then explain what happened and why.

The three of us walked out to the overview where I captured the most amazing pictures of Ian and Caroline. The snow, sky, mountains and clouds aligned, allowing the lens to capture the essence of their love. These pics would end up on Valentine's Day cards and travel brochures. I was sure the images would replace the rose as the symbol of two hearts intertwined as one.

As they finished the photo session, I started to get into position for them to return the favor when another love-smitten couple happened upon us. Being the kind, professional photographer that I am, I offered to use their phone to get some lifelong memories that would warm their hearts and adorn their fireplace mantle. As I returned their phone, I turned around, only to discover Ian and Caroline had taken off. I was stunned and speechless. In shock, and a little hurt by the bizarre behavior, I set off in pursuit and spotted them far off, going up a steep ascent before they disappeared into some trees. I caught up with them at the summit. I played coy. The views were so amazing it helped push the bad mojo out of my head. After our stay at the summit, I mentioned I wanted to stop off at the overview to have my picture taken. I scooted off ahead so I could get there first, take my gear off and get ready for my pics. Once there, I waited and waited. A man showed up, so I offered to take his picture. He confessed that his phone had died. I told him to give me his email and I would use my phone and send his photos later. He counter-offered to take my picture. I accepted, then started racing down the mountain realizing Ian and Caroline had hiked right past the overview and were heading down. What was going on? Why was this happening? I risked life and limb running down one of the steepest trails in New Hampshire to find them. Some hikers coming up informed me they had just passed a couple fitting their description a few hundred yards down trail. I took off running. I caught a glimpse of them rounding a switchback and yelled out to them. They didn't hear. Then it dawned on me ...

In their embarrassment of knowing they could never repay the photos I had taken of them, mixed with mild altitude sickness and dehydration, their behavior became characteristically uncharacteristic. I've seen it happen with Dave and Keith multiple times. Cannon is a very fatiguing hike and in the fog of exhaustion they had turned into mindless zombies. It becomes easy to forgive someone when you come to understand they suffer from a mental sickness.

When I finally caught up with them, the relaxed pace they were descending at, combined with the lowering elevation, had put them back into proper mental perspective. Even though their brain fart came up with a decoy excuse of not hearing me say I wanted to go back to the lookout, I was cool with it. Hey, that is what friends are for. Play it cool and never give people motives that are less pure than your own. Strange things can occur on winter hikes. We laughed it all away as I erased my original plans of a double homicide. After all, they were driving.

To prevent this from ever happening again, I think I will get a selfie stick.

Overall, this was a killer hike with perfect winter conditions. The beauty of the Whites is why people come from around the world to winter-hike here. That, and the rare chance they will run into me and get free, award-winning photos.

3 MOUNT LIBERTY
Solo Winter Hike

Dec. 29, 2021

Five days after hiking Cannon, the weather forecasts revealed ideal conditions for another winter hike. Because it fell on a Wednesday, none of the crew was able to go. I had been wanting to revisit Mount Liberty since my first time at the summit was socked in with low clouds obscuring the view. For some reason this peak kept beckoning to me, calling my name over and over. I decided it would be my first 4,000-footer winter solo. Darlene was concerned, but I assured her that being the only nice day in the forecast guaranteed there would be other hikers on the trail should anything happen.

I currently have no plans to complete the Winter 48. I get too cold. My finger and toes give me 10 reasons not to push my limits with sub-zero temps.

I did discover that the first to accomplish the Winter 48 were Robert (age 71) and Miriam (age 61) Underhill, in 1960. I received this piece of New Hampshire history from Mike Dickerman, who owns Bondcliff Books, a publisher and distributor in Littleton, N.H. He is the co-author with Steve Smith of *The 4000 Footers of the New Hampshire White Mountains.* Mike is a super-nice guy.

If I remember correctly, Mr. Underhill said he did not like Mrs. Underhill's cooking. What started as a room-to-room pursuit somehow morphed into a winter chase over all 48 peaks.

If you think that statistic is interesting, it gets even crazier. In 2019, Leah Lawry, Jason Beaupre and Andrew Soares completed the Winter 48 in 6 days, 21 hours and 4 minutes for the FKT (fastest known time).

While that is absolutely crazy, listen to this: I asked Darlene if we could watch our wedding video backwards. She asked why I would want to do that. I replied that I wanted to see myself leaving the church a free man. When she stopped chasing me on Day 5, I was 9 hours ahead of their record.

Seriously, marriage is great. My son once asked me what it is like being married. I told him to leave me alone. When he did, I asked him why he was ignoring me. Now he knows. Hahaha. They say you find the love of your life when you're not looking, but by then you have run her over. OK, I'll stop.

Mount Liberty is a 4,457-foot-high mountain in the White Mountains, overlooking Franconia Notch. It is part of Franconia Ridge, the second highest mountain group in the Whites after the Presidential Range. It lies south of Mount Lafayette, the highest summit along the ridge. It has a picturesque, jagged, bare rock summit unlike any other in New Hampshire.

Every now and then, the urge hits hikers to do a solo hike. When you hike with the clowns I hike with, the urge happens frequently. A perfect 24-hour window of nice weather opened up in an otherwise miserable pattern. It was forecasted to be sunny with temps in the mid-20's and winds at only 5 mph. I made a quick decision to jump at the opportunity and I am glad I did. It turned out to be the best hike ever. I decided to leave early as it was due to cloud over in the afternoon. Leaving at 4 a.m., I was the second car to arrive at the trailhead. The occupants of the other car must have been waiting for sunrise, which was not for an hour and a half. Not me. Putting on my headlamp and spikes I was the first on the trail. Hiking alone in the dark during the winter is awesome. I strongly recommend you try it at least once. As the sun rose, I ditched the headlamp. I had the entire hike up to myself. I did not encounter another hiker until just before summiting. A woman caught up to me and we summited together. At the summit, we met two other men and the three of them decided to head off for Mount Flume, leaving me alone on the peak where I spent the next 35 minutes in sheer bliss. I could have never imagined such spectacular views as the sun lit up peaks all around me. In my opinion, Liberty has the most impressive views in all of the Whites, and I was there alone to drink it all in. I took pics, panoramas and video. Clouds came crashing in from the southwest at around 3,500 feet. They slowly wrapped around the summit and created an undercast to the south allowing only the dark tips of surrounding 4,000-footers to appear through a blanket of white. To the north, Cannon, Lincoln and Lafayette were brilliantly glowing golden in the morning sun. I was like a kid in a candy store.

After some time, I stopped taking pictures, realizing the God-ordained beauty I was privileged to observe could not be stolen to an image. I took out my Thermos of coffee, sat on some rocks and lived the moment.

All things must end. A few hikers arrived and it was time to go. I bowed my head, thanked God for the gift I had enjoyed, put on my pack and started down. My heart was full.

On the journey of life, it is good to be truly thankful. There are three questions that haunt every person. Where did I come from? Why am I here? Where am I going? I have come to believe I was given life as a gift from God, that I am here to know Him and enjoy Him, and that through faith in Christ I receive eternal life. For me, it is the only conclusion that makes sense.

Back on the trail I started encountering lots of hikers heading up. There was one guy who was memorable. He was trail-running in crampons. Not spikes, but full-on crampons. He had already summited and now ran by me going down. His parting words were "I hope I don't get tripped up by a root." I do, too, crazy trail-running dude. I do, too.

Lesson of the Day: Sometimes you need alone time.

4 MOUNT ROBERTS
Winter Hike

Seems we are locked into a cold spell that will not quit. I love it when weather forecasters announce, "We are getting a cold front moving down from Canada." "Well, it sure as heck ain't coming up from Tennessee!" They also call these weather patterns a polar vortex. That is a nice way of saying it will be getting so cold your butt cheeks will freeze together and your teeth will chatter right out of your head while your lips turn blue. It boggles my mind to think I go out and hike in weather colder than my freezer. I am not into any other winter sports. I do not like the cold. I did see "Disney on Ice" once. What a letdown. It was an old guy in a freezer. (Darlene, don't edit that out, it's funny.)

On Sunday, Jan. 6, 2022, the temps shot up into the teens. Dave did not want to miss the window, so he suggested a late afternoon hike up a southerly mountain. As he is slowly working on his 52 With A View list, we decided on Mount Roberts in Moultonborough. The afternoon was all blue skies with hardly any wind. Dave, Keith, and I geared up and headed out.

My doctor had told me to lose weight. I asked how? "Don't eat anything fatty," he said. I asked, "Like pies and cake?" He said no, "Don't eat anything, fatty." So, having just started to shed weight, I did not want the crash that comes from being depleted of carbs, so I bought a chocolate chip muffin from Dunkin' that cost a half day's pay. I guess it is a combination of inflation and having to pay high school kids $18 an hour. I also brought along some candy to eat to assure I would have the needed energy to prevent bonking.

Mount Roberts is a great first hike. It is not long or steep and has great views. I have hiked it five or six times, each one in the winter. I keep promising that I will hike in the summer because it is a fun hike. Dave had made a New Year's resolution that he would be nicer to people. Especially us. Not believing it would last a week, Keith and I busted on him relentlessly to test his resolve. Surprisingly, he took it well and did not retaliate. I almost felt guilty. However, in time, the Old Dave started reappearing. He only lasted three days.

I had brought a Thermos of hot chocolate and shared some with Dave at the summit. As we began our descent, it was like rocket fuel inside of me. I was flying down the trail, and when the path gained elevation, I was actually running. A sugar-and-caffeine combination is a real thing! What a great winter hike. We came out to the parking lot just as the sun had set. Perfect timing.

"Don't eat anything, fatty." Haha, that cracks me up.

5 The Pemigewasset Search & Rescue Team

I was driving alone and lost in my thoughts during the two-hour ride north. Where had all this craziness begun? I started scrolling backwards through the last seven years of hiking memories. Living just a mile away from Pawtuckaway State Park with its three smaller mountains and miles of hiking trails presented the opportunity to escape the doldrums of the long, monotonous winter months. As a kid, I spent a fair share of time in the woods. Now, as an adult, the more I hiked the more I liked it. Winter hiking in Pawtuckaway was the genesis that led me into hiking my first 4,000-footer after a 20-year hiatus.

It started with Mount Waumbek. The story is found in my first book. Needless to say, that mountain ate my lunch and popped my brown paper bag. I hurt from my hair to my toenails. Every muscle in my body ached for days as I tried to evaluate what I had just done to myself. Being a funny guy, I decided to record the events of the hike and post it to my 700 followers on Facebook. People loved it. As I suffered through each hike, my followers were getting some laughs. The next thing I knew I had written two books on hiking and donated the profits to New Hampshire Search and Rescue.

Because of these events I had received an invitation to attend a Pemigewasset SAR meeting where I presented them with a donation. Dave went with me and we really enjoyed meeting the team. Sometime after that, I was invited by the vice president of the team, Jamie Bernard, to join him on his podcast called *It Sounds Like a Search and Rescue Call Is About to Happen*. Ian went with me and we had a blast sharing our stories with Mike and Stomp (Jamie).

Looking for new material to write a third (and final) book, I reached out to Jamie to ask if I could sit in on a meeting or training with the team. He threw a date at me and said they were going to be doing winter training on Mount Jackson and invited me to go along. I was pumped. This was going to be awesome. A few days before the hike, Jamie informed me he had the flu and would not be able to make it. Wait a minute! That is a typical Dave Salois move. Finding a reason to bail on a killer hike made me wonder if they secretly knew each other.

So here I am, driving north to meet the team and accompany them on a full-winter, simulated-rescue scenario, all the while pondering the fact that I may have gotten in over my head. What an understatement!!!

My plan was to enjoy six weeks of conditioning beforehand. Nay-nay. First, the weather would not cooperate. Second, my schedule blew up and I was as busy as a one-armed wallpaper hanger. Third, I got sick for 10 days. Fourth, I had a colonoscopy, which turned out to be the best prep I would receive for what was to come. It had been two months since my last hike and I was totally unconditioned.

The North Country had just received 17 inches of fresh snow two days before. This perfect Sunday morning was hard to resist and New Hampshire was being invaded by our Massachusetts friends. On the ride up, I passed a dead deer and a dead coyote, nature's way of warning me what was to come. Both prey and predator take a beating during our winter months.

I pulled into the AMC Highland Center to use the facilities, then drove 0.1 mile farther to the trailhead for Mount Jackson. The parking lot was full and cars were starting to park along Route 302. After sitting in my truck for 20 minutes I saw the first neon-green jacket of a SAR member. He introduced himself as Dan. He informed me that the team was assembling back at the Highland Center. Dan was a super-nice guy, and I would have gone with him but the walk there, then back again, was messing with the part of the brain called lazy. I told him I would just wait in my truck. About 45 minutes later I was wishing I had gone because I knew that in my absence, they conspired evil plans for ridding themselves of this pesky author who wanted to "hang out" with a highly trained band of hiking animals.

Although Mount Jackson is not named after the U.S. President, it is, along with Mount Webster, the start (from the south) of the Presidential Range. At only 4,052 feet, Jackson doles out 2,300 feet of elevation gain in 2.5 miles. In hiking terms, that's steeper than the cost of a Starbucks coffee. The entire range includes Webster, Jackson, Pierce, Eisenhower, Franklin, Monroe, Washington, Clay, Jefferson, Adams, and Madison. Hiking the whole thing in one day is called the Single-Day Prezi Traverse and there are freaks that actually enjoy doing it. This would be my third jaunt up Jackson. The first hike was in late spring with Keith, where I experienced the most god-awful wipeout I have ever taken. My legs were exhausted and I slipped off a wet rock. Instead of catching myself, my legs buckled like a Mini-Cooper colliding head-on into a Freightliner. The somersault that followed was not pretty. My second trip up was with Dave on Feb. 6, 2021. (To put this in perspective, my hike with the Pemi SAR was the exact same day a year later) Dave and I hiked in perfect winter weather. About a half a mile from the summit, we encountered a few hikers coming down that were crying and muttering suggestions that we should turn around. One apparently rugged guy just looked down and said, "It's brutal up there." We were kind of perplexed as it was 18° with no wind. As we approached the bare summit, we could hear what sounded like a jet engine. The 40-mph sustained wind was making the shelter of the last scant trees bend like wheat stalks in a hurricane. We moved out of the trees and into a flash freezer. Ninety seconds later I was heading down like Usain Bolt. Man was that cold. It was the first time I felt wind go through my Marmot Scree pants like I was wearing mosquito netting. I have heard it said it is only cold when you stop moving. That is a lie, I was moving fast and still freezing. My son had told me when your feet are cold, start flexing your butt cheeks. Somehow this pushes blood into your feet and toes. I had my butt cheeks jiggling like a fat lady in an earthquake, but nothing was happening.

I have since started using hand and toe warmers (not for my butt cheeks). I do not understand the science of how they work, I am just happy they do. Another joy of hiking in Antarctic weather is when you stop for a snack and crack two teeth biting into your Cliff bar. You know it is cold when you have to snap a piece off and let it thaw in your mouth before you can chew it. I knew my third hike up would be different. It had to be!

In my truck mirror I saw the convoy of neon green Pemi SAR jackets as the team was heading my way. After getting out of my truck and putting my pack on, I realized the winds that were blowing the clouds away were also bringing the wind chill down to about -3° F. I had already put toe warmers in my boots and hand warmers in my gloves. I heard my name called and made eye contact with a man who identified himself as Rusty. He was friendly with kind facial features. He informed me that he was the team leader and that while we would be hiking Jackson, we would not be summiting. I liked him right off.

Rusty gave instructions that we would stop at every junction to ensure the group stayed together. He double counted everyone to make sure no one would be left behind. Out of the 11 in the group, only four were wearing snowshoes. When I realized that most of them were going to bare-boot it, I was thrilled. I hate hiking in snowshoes. The monorail was compressed about 12 inches below the surface. The trail was somewhat soft. About 1.5 inches of loose snow made it feel like you were hiking in sand. Every now and then I would slip and that would prove to be exhausting.

My son belongs to the Tahoe Nordic Search and Rescue in Tahoe, Calif., and he had assured me teams do not usually hike fast on training exercises. Either he lied or I was now hiking with the A-Team of speed. What for them was a simple stroll up a hill quickly turned into a hike from hell for me. One of the team members said they thought they could hear the chugging of the Cog Railway engine ascending Mount Washington. I assured him it was my heart that was now pounding like a sledgehammer. The gang seemed to break up into three distinct groups. The first was four members who hiked fast and were leading the way. The second larger group appeared to be more moderate, and finally there were two lovely ladies who fell behind chatting and enjoying the day. Initially I was behind the first group. By the halfway mark I had fallen in with the second group, and within the last half mile I was with the two women who were slowing down for my sake. I offered to let them pass, but they were polite and said they didn't want to break up the team. I took that to mean a search-and-rescue team abandoning a heart-attack victim would not look good on the morning news. They were extremely kind and allowed me to stop to recover and even eat a candy bar. I think having women on a team is a great idea. After hiking with Keith, Dave and Ian, compassion was foreign to me.

As we trudged on, I mentioned to my two hiking angels how Rusty informed me we would not be summiting. They looked at each other and smiled and said, "No, we are definitely summiting." I gazed upward and a quarter mile away I could see the bare rock dome of the summit. Rusty lied! Why would anyone do that to a nice, lovable guy like me? The day after the hike, I contacted Jamie and requested Rusty's pay be cut in half. Jamie reminded me that Rusty, as do all the volunteers, serves for free. I then suggested he lose half his freedom.

The last push to the summit is incredibly steep. The rock was covered in ice and loose snow. It is a real wakeup call, as you hit the 4,000-foot marker, how the temps drop drastically. The ladies were stopping to put on another layer. Rusty came down to meet me and gave me some advice on navigating the last, horrible stretch of trail. It was messing with my head. Good cop, bad cop? I did not know what to think about this guy. The team was standing around on top in 25 mph winds like they were at Hampton Beach in the summer. It was so cold, my nose froze and my sinuses were actually hurting. I think the game plan was to get this green horn to the summit, then freeze those horns blue. They were not the only thing turning blue. My male parts had retreated internally to the warmth of my spleen, my butt cheeks froze together, and my piggy toes felt like they were hung in a meat freezer. I removed my mitts to snap some pictures only to discover that my new Stoic puffy mitts, after getting wet with sweat, were almost impossible to get back on. I sure wish I had not experimented with new gear on the hike. I know that severe hypothermia can lead to frostbite and possible amputation. I am really happy that today's prosthetics are so advanced that most people can go on to live a productive life. It is not like it was in pirate days when they were left with a wooden peg-leg, a hook and an eye patch. Once a young lad questioned a pirate on how he got his peg-leg. The pirate answered with "Well, lad, it was a broadside cannon ball, took me leg clean off." The youngster then asked about the hook, the reply was "'Twas a swashbuckler sword fight, cut me hand right off." Then in youthful curiosity the boy asked about the eye patch. The pirate gruffly responded, "'Twas a seagull that pooped right in my eye." The boy in amazement asked, "And that caused you to lose your eye?" "Don't be daff," the pirate said, "It was the first day with me new hook."

I somehow managed to get Rusty's attention by jumping up and down, waving my arms in the air and crying like a teen who just lost phone privileges. Rusty agreed the temps were a bit chilly and the group headed down. I was following two team members who were in snowshoes. When we hit the ice, they went down like bowling pins. Just as I was thankful I was not wearing snowshoes, I followed suit by slipping, falling, and butt-sliding. As long as I was going down, I did not care. I do not know if anyone else slipped because I never looked back. I ended up falling again. Some nice team members asked if I needed a hand up. I declined. I was trying to hang on to a shred of dignity. It was sad. I somehow ended up in the lead position. I was going fast and the trail was so steep, that at times I was skiing with spikes on. The combination of walking fast, skiing, slipping and sliding, then back to walking fast, set my quads on fire. By relying heavily on my hiking poles my shoulders felt like they were popping out of socket. After the first half mile of descending, I surrendered first place and took up next to last. The only reason I was not last was because Rusty and another gentleman insisted on remaining behind to not break up the group. Secretly, I knew they were keeping an eye on me, expecting this to become a full-blown rescue at any moment.

Our rendezvous was at the junction to the Webster branch of the Webster-Jackson Trail. It was a long way off and my thoughts had turned dark. Pain clouded my mind. I was pondering how these people could hike so fast in these crappy conditions. Then it dawned on me: isn't that what everyone counts on when in danger? The faster, the better. They do this stuff constantly for no pay or reward other than the thanks from other hikers. This was a Sunday afternoon when weekend warriors were here to enjoy skiing, ice climbing and hiking, and these folks were out doing training to keep their skills sharp for those who may be in need. Sure, my shoulders hurt, and my legs felt like they were falling off, but I was in the company of heroes. I am betting when someone injures themselves or gets lost, those neon-green jackets are the best sight their eyes will ever see. I know some people think I am crazy donating the profits of my books to NH SAR.

All I can recommend is to spend some time with these people. Talk to someone who got carried out after an injury. These teams are, in my opinion, a true band of brothers and sisters and I, for one, am very thankful for all of them. And it is not just the Pemigewasset SAR. The long list includes New Hampshire Fish and Game, the Androscoggin Valley SAR, Lakes Region SAR, Upper Valley Wilderness Response Team, Mountain Rescue Services, New England K9 SAR, White Mountain Swiftwater Rescue Team, Mount Washington Volunteer Ski Patrol, Appalachian Mountain Club, Dartmouth-Hitchcock Advanced Response Team, and the New Hampshire Army National Guard medevac units. In my humble opinion, they are all an amazing group of givers who make up what is best about America.

Back at the trail junctions, the SKED training began.

On the official Skedco website, under FAQs, you will find the answer to "What does "SKED" stand for?"

"Though we spell it with capital letters, SKED is not an acronym. It came from fusing two words: "Skid and Sled." The early idea behind the product was that it was a SLED that SKIDDED across all types of terrain. Initially, the SKED was used as a game carrier to tote wild game back to a hunter's camp. It has since morphed into the lifesaving device that's used today all across the globe. Like many iconic products that are the first of its kind in the market, the brand has come to epitomize the thing itself."

The SKED is a bright orange piece of plastic. After opening it up, a wool blanket is placed on it, followed by a sleeping pad. The patient is placed on it, bundled up and slid down the mountain to a waiting ambulance. The team members were saying, "Ken, get in, be our patient." At first, I was, like, all down with it saying "sure." I thought it would be fun. Someone humorously referred to the SKED as the "Bosse Bag." I hope that does not catch on. As they started wrapping me up, I started getting a creepy feeling of claustrophobia. They were all very understanding and insisted it was not for me as they witnessed my shaking body, quivering lips and tears. I believe I may have peed myself. I sure wish Dave had been hiking with me. I would have loved to have seen him strapped in and immobilized, especially with a mitt jammed in his mouth. I asked one of the women if they have drugs to give someone like me to knock me out. She replied they do not do that. WOW! That puts me in a quandary. Do I let them put me in that thing or die on the trail? I hope I never have to find out. I believe my best course of action would be to talk one of the members into hiking out to Gorham, score some downers, dope me into yesterday, bundle me up like a newborn baby and slide me down the mountain. Yup, that is what I'm going to do!

Another volunteer stepped in and I watched the training with wide-eyed excitement. (In the picture you can see how tightly he is strapped in.)

There were some members who were making sure he was warm and comfortable, while others were tying ropes that would allow members to pull the SKED uphill and others to hold it back from taking off like a luge. All of this took time, but I was enthralled. That is, until I started freezing. After sweating like I had, standing around for 40 minutes took its toll. I also noticed the time. It was 3 p.m. I still had an hour hike out and a two-hour drive home. I thanked Rusty and the team for a great adventure and headed out solo. On my way out I had another memorable fall that ended up in a 25-foot butt slide. The last mile out seemed like it would never end. Because I had parked directly across from the trailhead, I spotted my truck when I was still a few hundred feet in the woods. The feeling was euphoric. I was now wondering if I had the leg strength to operate the pedal. I was feeling like Waumbek all over again, but this time it was well worth it.

The drive home was the worst part of the day. All those out-of-state visitors were headed home, and I got stuck in a 10-mile traffic jam that caused my two-hour ride home to take 3 1/2 hours. Oh well. All in all, it still turned out to be an amazing day.

Thank you, Jamie. Thank you, Rusty. Thank you, Pemigewasset Search and Rescue.

You are amazing.

P.S.: Next time you need a volunteer for, let's say, a cliff rescue, I know Ian would love the opportunity.

6 It's Raining Cats & Dogs

Animals are starting to make a huge appearance on the trails these days. Some of them are even bringing their cats and dogs. I have no opinion either way. I have brought goldfish on many hikes. Cheddar flavor is my favorite. I have been accused of hiking with monkeys, but I refuse to let people treat my hiking companions that way. Seriously, growing up, my family always had animals. Dogs, cats, horses, chickens, lambs — even a domesticated crow. Both my parents grew up on farms in northern Maine where animals were a part of life. As a young boy, when one of our favorite dogs died, my dad said he would get us an identical one. "What will we do with two dead dogs?" I asked. I kicked a dog once and it bit me. Darlene said, "It's karma." I said, "No, if anything it's angrier." (It is tough being 63 with a 10-year-old mind, but someone has to do it.)

I remember a Reader's Digest article about a man who was a martial arts expert and got attacked by two large dogs. (True story.) He fought them off as best as he could, but he tired before they did, and he had to retreat by climbing a nearby tree. He was torn up pretty bad. Those dogs would have killed anyone else. Stories like that stay with me. Note to dog lovers: when Cuddles is growling at me with lips curled showing fangs, please do not inform me that he is harmless. I call BS. There are dogs that I trust and those I do not. Once, while hiking in Pawtuckaway, I heard a noise coming from the woods. Off trail! I thought it was a deer. Suddenly two large black dogs appeared and came at me full speed while barking aggressively. It happened to be one of the only times I was carrying a side arm and instinctively my hand dropped down to it. I do like dogs, so I gave them the benefit of the doubt. One dog turned about 10 feet in front of me and the other clipped my leg as it ran past, slightly knocking me off balance. The owner came running, apologizing profusely. I get it, things happen. Most dogs are super friendly and the worst thing you experience are muddy paw prints as they jump up on you. It's all good. Having listed some negatives, let me touch on the positives. Dogs are awesome. No one loves you like a dog. They are always happy to see you and love spending time with you. They are faithful and constant companions. They do not complain as you pour your heart out to them and always listen while wagging their tails in delight. They are gifts from heaven. Cats, on the other hand, are demon spawns with attitudes from hell. Some animal researchers, after studying large cats, said the normal house cat has probably thought of killing you at one time or another. You can see it in their eyes. If you are a cat lover, roll with it. You know there is an element of truth to it. I know of one cat lover who is summiting all 48 4,000 footers with her feline friend. I am 100 percent in favor of that. I mean, sure, whatever.

I went hiking with a guy who bought his Doberman. The thing was the size of a moose.

The first thing the dog did after hitting the trail was to take a mammoth dump right in the middle of the trail. I would have been duly impressed had it not been for the fact that it took another four of equal size, all dead center on the trail. I was stupefied at the amount of crap that dog could eliminate while reminding myself never to visit the guy's backyard. I speculated if he were ever to bag his dog's poop on a trail, he would need a 10-gallon Hefty.

The dog would take off, causing his owner to yell, whistle, and scream for the four-legged septic system to return. When it did, Fido would stick around for 10 seconds then disappear again, resulting in more yelling. That process did not stop for the whole five-mile hike. Aarghhhhhhh!

My neighbor came up to me and asked why I put superglue on his dog? I said, "You just can't let it go, can you?" Did you know there are dogs that can actually smell if you have cancer? Good news is, if it senses you only have a year to live, it is really seven.

I am all for support animals. I believe all things given to us are good, including animals, especially when they can help someone through a tough time.

Here is a list of emotional support animals that people have brought with them on airplanes: squirrels (won't they make you feel nuts?); ducks (that quacks me up); kangaroos (if they cannot make you feel better, they will kick the crap out of you); miniature horse (on an airplane?); capuchin monkey (why not?); pigs; turkeys; domestic goats; turtles (if you are getting emotional support from a turtle, you have bigger problems than you know. They will never help you come out of your shell); and last, but not least, ... hedgehogs. You just know it is only a matter of time before you run into a hedgehog on Bondcliff Mountain.

Getting back to reality: the American Kennel Club recommends these breeds for best hiking companion: Siberian Husky, Australian Shepherd, German Shorthaired Pointer, Vizsla, Australian Cattle Dog, Weimaraner, Bernese Mountain Dog, Rhodesian Ridgeback, Alaskan Malamute, or Portuguese Waterdog. Remember, just like you, your dog will need hydration and extra food while on a mountain excursion. For cat lovers, there is a great website called *Adventure Cats* that can walk you through all you will need to know about hiking with your cat. There is also a nice site called "Oh crap," for when your fury four-legged friends encounter wildlife and come running home to you with a pissed off 400-pound black bear on their heels. Your dog may stick around to defend you, but that cat is going to throw you under the bus!

Oh well, happy tails ... I mean, trails.

7 First Overnighter

Camping is a magical word. It paints imaginative pictures of fun and adventure. You automatically see yourself sitting in front of your tent by a nice fire, sipping coffee, while the sun sets over the horizon. Peepers chirp a melodious bedtime lullaby as you crawl into a soft sleeping bag that is just the right temperature for a night of blissful rest. You awake refreshed the next morning, not having stirred once in the night. The fire's embers are still warm as new fuel ignites, heating a fresh cup of coffee as you greet the warm sunrise of a new day. Heck, that sounds so wonderful I can't wait to go.

This is what really happens: You are exhausted, sweaty and sore from hiking 11 miles on a grueling trail with a heavy pack. You set up camp quickly because it looks like it might rain. You forgot half your tent stakes, so the tent sags rather than being taunt, plus your shelter for the night is at a 10-degree pitch because you cannot find level ground anywhere! You do not have a fire because they are not allowed. You are not sitting outside your tent because mosquitoes the size of hummingbirds would carry you off and suck you dry in two minutes. Peepers and tree frogs are making an ungodly racket that is louder than a rock concert, and the soft sleeping bag has three stones and a root the size of a redwood underneath it. It is not the right temperature because it never is and never will be. You are either trying to sleep in a sticky sauna or you are shivering so bad your teeth rattle while the moisture from your breath forms icicles on the ceiling of your sagging tent. You do not "wake up," because you never really fell asleep. You are not refreshed. If fact, you no longer even feel human. The sun is not rising because it is overcast and raining. The dampness will not allow your stove to light so that morning coffee is cold with pine needles in it. OK! Who wants to go?

Dave and I had been itching to get out and do an overnighter. We both had bought a ton of gear we never got a chance to use. The weather was cool enough for camping without needing a tent to shield you from demon mosquitoes. We agreed upon the perfect location, packed up and headed out. Our plan was to hike a mountain, camp at a shelter, then hike another mountain the next morning. The shelter was a one-mile hike, all uphill. After hiking the first peak, the walk to the shelter was brutal. We arrived at sunset, set out our sleep systems, had dinner and settled in for the night.

The shelter was large and fairly new. The one thing that caught us off guard was a bottle of disinfectant spray and a sign on the wall that said, "After use of the shelter, please disinfect it according to CDC guidelines against Covid." WTH? Seriously? We had driven six miles down a dirt road, then hiked another mile into nothing but wilderness. We were in an open three-sided shelter miles away from anyone and someone wants us to disinfect a wide-open shelter?? Welcome to the new normal.

Most people can sleep through the night. Not me. I have a bladder the size of a walnut and need to get up three times a night to tinkle. There I was, headlamp on, relieving myself, hearing the sounds of the forest (and Dave's snoring) wondering if Covid had stalked us to the far reaches of the northern New Hampshire wilderness. After a restless night, I awoke before sunrise and waited for Sleeping Beauty to wake up.

When it became apparent that he would sleep till noon, I set up my stove and made my breakfast and coffee. Like a sleeping dog that jumps up at the sound of the refrigerator door opening, Dave was suddenly wide awake. He really is a weirdo.

I suggested we head out in the dark and see if we could catch a sunrise on our second peak. Dave was all energy. I was not. On the hike up, Dave pulled away and soon vanished. I was alone with my thoughts and the dim illumination of my headlamp. I spotted a blowdown along the way that looked to be the perfect place to sit and recover. As I sat in exhaustion, Mr. Slept Like A Baby jumped out from behind a giant pine tree right across the trail from where I sat. I would have been scared out of my mind had I had any energy. His little sadistic ploy backfired, amusing me greatly. After stumbling and bumbling we finally summited and were met with a gray socked-in view. Still, our first overnighter proved to be successful. It would become the new goal for hiking.

Two notes of interest: First, I will never share where we camp. Like a fisherman who never reveals his favorite spots, or a hunter who will not reveal his secrets, our camping locations remain classified. Second, you will never hear of Keith camping out with us. He is still pretty sour about our night out while hiking the Bonds. The story is found in my first book. We are all sympathetic with his decision because, at his age, getting a good night's sleep is really all you have left.

8 Second Overnighter

Dave and I selected a location that required a four-mile hike in. By the time he got off work, and the travel time, we calculated we would do half the hike with fading daylight and the other half with the aid of our headlamps. We stopped at Subway, purchased our dinner and headed north. Everything went as planned. Setting up camp in the dark is a skill best left for experienced mountain men. This time there was no shelter. We set up our sleep systems under the stars. There are four choices that can be made for a campout experience. First is the use of an AMC shelter, typically a three-sided log construction. Second is the use of a tent. Third, cowboy camp under the stars, and fourth, to sleep in a $25,000 pull-behind camper with A/C, heat, kitchen, bathroom and queen-sized bed, like Keith does. Age has privilege.

After rummaging around like a couple of raccoons, looking for the perfect level spot, Dave and I set up our sleep systems. Sleep system is a term that sounds cool and makes people think you know what you are talking about. For me, it includes a two-inch-thick air pad. After blowing the dang thing up you will discover you are so lightheaded you are ready to sleep. Air pads are psychological sales tricks, fooling you into believing you will be getting a restful night's sleep. Second, underneath the air pad, I place a foam ground pad. It really adds extra comfort and is lighter than dragging a six-inch mattress around. Next is the actual sleeping bag. Bags are priced by temperature ratings created by Eskimos. For example, a zero-degree bag means that at 0° F you will most likely survive and not die from hypothermia. The comfort rating really means at 15° you will freeze your buns off and wish you would die. At 30° you will probably get a half night's decent sleep. Be forewarned. However, a summer bag rating means you will sweat no matter what and you'll probably drown in your soaking-wet bag. The clothing you sleep in also affects how warm or cool you will be. Experiencing a perfect night's sleep while camping is as rare as seeing Bigfoot being levitated by a light beam from a flying saucer. The last item to a sleep system is an air pillow. The first time I used one I blew it up a little too much and became an instant bobblehead. Letting out some air revealed that a good air pillow is an invaluable purchase. And there you have it — "sleep systems."

Dave and I admired the star-filled sky, ate a few snacks, and then crawled into our sleeping bags. At around 11:30 p.m., I awoke for my normal nighttime pee. While snuggling back into my warm bag I noticed my phone. I don't know why these thoughts come into my brain, but I found myself calling Dave, who was lying 8 feet away from me. I couldn't help giggling as I heard his phone ringing, then heard his groggy voice say, "Elloooo." I simply said, "Dave, stop snoring," and hung up.

We awoke to a sunrise that was simply stunning. The spectacular views were constantly changing as the sun climbed higher in the sky. We took loads of pictures.

Hunger settled in and it was time for breakfast. We dug out our stoves from our packs and went to work. I use a Jetboil cooking system. (See what I did there? System?)

The Jetboil is a self-contained system where all the components fit inside the cooking pot. The fuel canister, stove, stand, with pot, all in one unit. I filled it with water and within a few minutes it was boiling, thus the name, Jetboil. Next, I opened my Mountain House freeze-dried "Breakfast Scrambler" meal, poured the boiling water in and, presto, instant awesomeness. I gave some to Dave, who upon trying it immediately spat it out saying, "I'm not a fan." I was flabbergasted. They are delicious. He said it was the consistency he didn't like. Really? Consistency? Sorry for the delicate palate. Oh well, it was a two-serving packet, so I enjoyed a hearty breakfast. Ian, unlike Dave, loves these things. I have had numerous Mountain House meals and have yet to find one I did not like. While consuming breakfast, my coffee was brewing. Man, oh man, there is nothing like a hot breakfast with coffee after a campout, accompanied by an epic sunrise.

While driving home, Dave was questioning why my phone took clearer pictures than his as they were identical phones. I asked, "Did you remove the clear plastic film they placed over the camera lens for protection?" Knowing there is no protective film, I watched in hysterics as he squinted his eyes and gently scratched with his fingernail. As I busted out laughing, he slid his phone back into his pocket. For the next six miles, he stared out the passenger side window and never said a word. Hahaha, that's rich.

My father once famously said of his three sons that "You were born shitheads and you will die shitheads!" I cannot remember what antic we had done to deserve that epithet, but Dave is beginning to understand.

9 Third Overnighter
Total Fail

Ian was becoming envious of our overnighters. As we planned another event, he was all in. This would again require a night hike to the location, followed by setting up with the aid of headlamps. It would not go as planned. As we drove north, Ian and Dave were spellbound over hearing stories of my mountain experiences. As usual, their masked, jealousies came out in statements such as "Would you please shut up? We are trying to listen to Lord Huron."

The hike in was lonely as they kept falling behind the pace I was setting. We arrived at our destination to discover there were no suitable places to camp. It ended with the three of us sleeping on the trail. First Dave, then some rocks, Ian and some more rocks, then me. This was not an ideal situation as the twists and turns, ups and downs of the trial offered a lousy foundation to sleep on. Also, this is a "no-no" hiker move because hikers coming in early get really upset when the trail is obstructed by sleeping morons. We had no alternative. We knew we would be up by 4 a.m. and we knew fog and drizzle in the forecast would keep most other hikers home. We ate dinner, sat out for a while, then turned in. What a miserable night. Fog brought dew that was getting everything wet. Ian's air mattress made squeaking sounds like butt cheeks moving around in a bathtub. My night was spent in a fitful attempt to sleep. At one time I must have dozed off because I was awakened by the sniffing sound of a bear checking out my backpack. I jolted up while yelling, "No you don't!" Ian and Dave groggily asked what was going on. It was then I realized that what I thought was a bear's sniffing sound was more likely the soft scratching sound of a mouse after snacks. I told the goons to never mind, I had scared it off, without ever having to define "it."

I read recently that the phrase "Good morning" dates back to the 1500's and is found in multiple languages. I am not sure it is used much by campers. My eyes opened to the realization I was somewhere, but not at all sure where. At first, I thought it was a nightmare, where I was sleeping in a wet sleeping bag in the middle of a rock-strewn trail in the Whites. As the mental fog lifted and the real fog soaked me, it dawned on me that was exactly where I was. Ian and Dave started waking up due to me loudly complaining. There were no "good mornings." Not even "morning." If fact, all we were doing was grunting, rubbing our eyes and assessing the situation. How did I let these goons talk me into camping at a non-previously-scoped-out campsite? We retrieved our stoves and got breakfast going as we packed up our wet sleep systems. As the veiled sun rose, the fog lifted, and things quickly dried. We consumed a nice hot breakfast while checking out some higher elevation views.

There is another phrase that says, "It still beats being at work." NO, it does not. When hiking, you learn to embrace everything as the overall experience. This was one of those times. You may not hit a home run every time, but at least you still got up to bat. Hikes like this one become war stories, but at least they are still stories.

As the saying goes, "If you can't crap with the big dogs, don't run with the pack."

10 Training with NH Fish & Game
Mt. Cardigan Winter Hike

I had the good fortune of meeting Lt. James Kneeland of New Hampshire Fish and Game at a Pemigewasset SAR meeting more than a year ago. Kneeland is in charge of the officers who oversee all the SAR events that happen in the state. I had reached out to ask him if there was a meeting I could attend to observe their organization as I wanted to share information in this book about their work. He responded, letting me know they were having a winter training session in a few weeks and invited me to come along. I was as happy as a Hollywood actress who took her meds. The events that followed were epic. Here is the truth of what happened.

I had gone on a training exercise the week before with the Pemigewasset SAR up Mount Jackson. Two days before that event, we had received 17 inches of fresh snow. The hike was brutal. It had since warmed up, making conditions slushy, followed by a miraculous deep freeze, making conditions perfect for hiking in spikes for traction. No snowshoes needed! A quick check on Mountain Forecast revealed the cold snap was to be accompanied by 30 mph winds on the summit, lowering the temps to -15°. I was madder than an angry bull watching a fat man walk by dressed in red. This winter has been completely uncooperative! Temperatures that cold are way below my personal comfort level.

I picked Keith up and drove an hour and a half to the AMC Cardigan Lodge. We arrived to find seven or eight Fish and Game officers getting their gear together. One officer had an accident and needed to leave to see a doctor for an eye injury. I caught up with Lt. Kneeland as another eight officers were pulling in and he went over the plans with me. I had to wonder, after realizing that every one of them backed into their parking space, what they knew that I did not. My truck was the only one nose in. Is that a law enforcement thing? Were they expecting a quick getaway from an alien invasion or was it just Keith? This parking pattern was an enigma.

These guys had gargantuan packs weighing in at 60 to 70 pounds. They carried all their rescue gear such as avalanche shovels, 12-foot probing poles, radios, beacons, crampons, survival gear, food and hydration. Because they would be spending the night at High Cabin, they also carried extra clothing, complete sleep systems, stoves and fuel. My pack looked impressive, but it was mostly clothing to keep my buns from freezing off. The only other guy I know whose pack weighs around 40 pounds would be Dave, and 25 pounds of that are just hand warmers.

There were 15 officers, with Keith and I bringing the number to 17. Kneeland assembled everyone together, made some quick introductions, gave the agenda for the day, and we were off. Keith and I were first on the trail, but we were soon passed by two officers. They hit the Manning Trail junction and stopped. We walked past them, took the Manning Trail for about 100 feet and stopped. Then another two joined the first two and stopped. I moved farther down the trail watching. Finally, a couple more joined in, and they all decided that the Manning Trail, the one we had taken, was the right trail. It starts moderate, gets steep, then hits the ledges after 1.2 miles. The trail condition was hard-packed snow, perfect for spikes. After a while, I stopped for a breather and asked the six officers if they had read any of my books. They had not. I explained that my books are humorous, and I usually pick on people. I then offered if they could collectively come up with $20, I would not mention the debacle I just witnessed at the trail junction. They immediately blamed it on their superiors who had fallen behind and were not there to instruct them. We laughed and I knew we were going to have a great day.

Because the forecast was Arctic cold, I wore a base layer under my Marmot scree pants. I usually never do that as it can be hot to hike in. Though I did sweat a little, I was happy to have them on while we stood motionless for 45 minutes. I also slid into my L.L. Bean 850 fill down jacket and my snowmobile mitts with large hand warmers in them. I was fairly toasty. Out of fear of turning into a popsicle I had also brought my full winter (non-hiking) jacket that drops down to my knees. Though I never wore it, it was nice to know I had more layers to count on. My Thermos of hot chocolate was like the nectar of the gods.

The training began with the use of beacons to find avalanche victims. The thought of being buried in an avalanche keeps me well away from any areas that could produce one. Avalanches are no joke. In 2020, 37 people died in avalanches in the U.S. Anyone who hikes, or backcountry skis, should get training in reading the terrain. Avalanches move fast. It is not just about being buried alive, it is about being swept downwards at speeds of 80 to 100 mph into rocks and trees. Wearing a beacon and an inflating vest can save your life. Swimming when caught in one can also help you move closer to the surface. What most people do not realize is that the chemistry of snow changes as it tumbles downward, making that soft, puffy snow solidify into cement. Even if your head and one arm were free above the snow, chances are you could not dig yourself out. Most survivors know the importance of creating an air pocket in front of their face as the avalanche slows to a stop. The average survival time is two to three hours, although the longest report is of someone surviving 22 hours after being buried. That must have been as terrifying as watching *Sleepless in Seattle*.

Observing the team train with beacons was amazing. How the beacons work, as well as the process of finding the center of the signal, was new to me. After the lesson, the men went on simulated searches over the cliffs, tracking beacon signals. Most beacons can send a signal anywhere from 130 to 260 feet, so that is why it is important if you see someone get swept in an avalanche to maintain eye contact, tracking where you believe they have stopped. Narrowing the location is crucial. Beacons are electronic devices, so most manufacturers recommend replacing them every three to four years. I started getting signals from Keith that he was getting cold, so I turned off my beacon-complaint receiver.

Next was the use of probing poles to locate someone under the snow. Probes are made from aluminum or carbon fiber. Though carbon fiber is lighter, the aluminum poles tend to be longer and sturdier to penetrate the hard snow. The poles the team carried seemed to be around 10 to 12 feet high. Probes are usually used by a number of searchers in a straight-line formation in order that every two feet of area is covered. It is all about finding a person in the fastest way possible. There are also trained dogs that are sometime used to sniff out a person's location. If Ian ever gets caught in an avalanche, all he would have to do is cut one and a dog could find him in a square mile. When located, the digging starts. The main objective is to locate the person and move as quickly as possible to uncover their face so that breathing is unobstructed, then dig out the rest of their body. My son had two friends in Tahoe, Calif., who were each, at different times, buried and then quickly recovered. Both had the same reaction: as soon as they were uncovered, they barfed and then cried like babies. I can only imagine I would do the same. Dang avalanches!

These officers trained hard under cold conditions, and we should all be thankful. Not only that, but their bright-red jackets made them look rather impressive. I need to interject that my down jacket is bright orange, making me fit right in with the dress of the officers. I did not fit in exactly, being much more handsome than anyone in that group. Keith was now so cold I could hear his teeth chattering through his sobs. Then in the same tone my grandson uses he said, "Can we go now?"

Before Keith and I headed off we were told the funniest story of a rescue. Four hikers had gotten lost on Firescrew Mountain and called for help. Just so happens, in the valley below there is a gentleman who raises hybrid wolves. As dusk approaches they can get rather noisy. Seems our wayward fab-four heard the howling and imagined the worst. I cannot say I blame them. When the responding officer arrived in their vicinity, he smelled smoke. Turns out they felt they would be safer with a fire. Unfortunately, their fire-starting skills were weak, and they had burned every piece of paper they could find trying to start a fire. They were down to burning money. The main contributor to their effort was relieved when the officer showed up. In gratitude, he said, "Thank goodness you are here, I went through all my ones, fives and tens, and only had twenties left."

And you thought hiking was an inexpensive hobby.

Keith and I headed off to Cardigan as the Fish and Game crew had another 20 minutes of training to go. We took our time to minimize sweating. The ridge walk over is a beautiful journey in and out of scattered small trees and wide-open space. I have always loved the open area of Firescrew Mountain. The last push to Cardigan is rather steep and the wind was ripping. Temperatures with wind chill were -15°. That is around 30° below my comfort zone. I find it amazing that people love hiking in this stuff. At the summit, we found shelter at the base of the fire tower. Winds were around 30 mph, with gusts up to 40 mph. I finished my hot chocolate, then headed to the summit edge to observe tiny red dots as the officers' jackets glowed against the white snow. Within 20 minutes, they had finally all assembled by the tower. I told them I was getting so concerned about how late they were I was about to call SAR. They got a kick out of that.

It was time for some group pictures. It was so cold that I had now doubled-hooded myself. I took my mitts off and got into position. I had wanted to get in the group photo with them, but I just cannot trust the goons I hike with to take a respectable picture. With my mitts removed, my hands were freezing up faster than some of the girls I asked out on dates. Finally, with hardly any mobility left in my fingers the crew was all grouped up, and I blasted off around 10 pics. Everyone was pretty cold, so Kneeland asked if I could email him the shots. Keith and I thanked them all and bolted down to treeline to get out of that incessant wind. The Clark Trail side of the summit is pretty steep, but it was all covered in hard-packed snow and our spikes gave us the grip we needed. Within a few minutes, we were in the trees and the temps were noticeably warmer just by being out of the wind. About halfway down, we met a lone officer coming up. His child was sick, so he was late to the party, but still wanted to get together with the group. Being an Afghanistan veteran, he was confident that his 70-pound pack was better than what he carried in the military. He assured us nothing weighs more than guns and ammo. As we parted ways, I asked him if he would let Lt. Kneeland know the pics I took would be $10 each. He laughed and promised me he would.

A little farther down we met two elderly gentlemen coming up, so we stopped and chatted for a while. They were both very friendly. After 10 minutes of chewing the fat, we said our goodbyes and headed out. Both Keith and I reminisced about the great time we had just had. Our time spent with the team of officers from Fish and Game was revealing of the rigors they go through to save lives and informative of the techniques and tools they use during a rescue. Whether it is kayakers, 4-wheelers, skiers, hikers or hunters, these guys, supported by all the SAR teams in New Hampshire, are our guardian angels. Thank you, Lt. Kneeland for the invitation, and thank you team for allowing us to tag along. I hope Keith was not too much of a bother.

Please go to the New Hampshire Fish and Game website and look into purchasing a Hike Safe card. They are $25 each or $35 for a family and can save you the cost of being charged for a rescue should you ever need one. www.wildlife.state.nh.us

11 Jennings Peak & Sandwich Mountain
Winter Hike

I am sure you have heard the phrase "when hell freezes over." If it did not happen this winter, then it never will. I mean, I bet even Satan put on some long johns. I recently read an article called "Forest Bathing" by Eric H. Hoyer, a certified arborist and forester. Seems that spending just 20 minutes in the woods can lower blood pressure, increase a sense of ease, boost immune systems, speed up surgery recovery, alleviate depression, improve sleep, increase blood to the brain and create more mental energy. I do not doubt any of that, but I am going to go out on a limb and guess that forest bathing is best done above 50° F — otherwise all bets are off!

Keith, Ian, Dave and I had made plans to hike Jennings Peak and Sandwich Dome. The temp with wind chill was going to be -15°. When I share stories with friends about winter hikes, I often hear, "That is way too cold for me." I wholeheartedly agree. My temperature sweet spot for hiking is between 40° and 60° F. Single digits and below is a bit frosty, though I will hike in the cold if there are no other options. I have a friend who moved to Arizona. When he tells me it is 113° F, I tell him he is nuts. He usually responds, "But it's a dry heat." What the heck does that mean? One hundred thirteen is 113! Next time someone tells me -5° is way too cold for me, I am going to tell them, "Ya, but it's a dry cold." Anyway, the night before the hike, Ian said he could not go. Early the next morning Dave said he was not feeling well. After conferring with Keith, he said he wanted to pass as well. I never hold it against them even if they are a bunch of wimps.

The next week, we all planned on attempting the hike again. Thursday and Friday the temps warmed up, then Friday night they dropped to single digits. We were delighted. That meant the snow would soften up, then freeze solid and we could hike with spikes and not cumbersome snowshoes. We were all pretty excited, got up early and rallied at our meeting place. We stopped to get some bagels and drove north. Conditions were as expected. We ditched our snowshoes and headed up the Sandwich Mountain Trail. Early on, there was a river crossing and we were confronted with a swollen river that was not only flowing under the ice, but because of the melt the days before, was now flowing over the ice as well. We bushwhacked up- and downstream looking for a safe place to cross. It never materialized. A few times I ventured out onto the ice and stomped down with my foot, only to break through into slush. We tried another trail that went farther up where the river was divided, yet even with the smaller tributary we were confronted with an impassible river. Here is the dilemma: even if you could cross, the temps later in the day were warming back up and while hiking for four hours it is not unrealistic that we would return to find the river wider and deeper. That is how some people find themselves stuck on the wrong side of a swollen river and have to call for a rescue. We decided the safest alternative was to call it quits. The mountains will always be there. Please exercise caution and stay safe, people.

We decided to drive farther north and hike into the Flume Gorge. I have lived in New Hampshire all my life and have never seen it. Call me cheap, but there is something about paying a hefty entrance fee to see nature. During the winter you do not have to pay, but there is a sign that reads "Enter at your own risk." We hiked in with the aid of spikes. There was a lot of ice. The trail going right into the gorge was blocked off, but the trail allowed you to go up and around it. In the canyon we discovered ice climbers ascending walls of sheer ice. Leaving there, we hiked the loop, then it began snowing heavily. I love hiking while it is snowing. It is just a great feeling. As we neared the parking lot, we started meeting whole groups of people hiking in with dress boots and sneakers. Ian pointed out a woman and told me she was wearing a $1,000 Canadian Goose jacket. I said, "Wait till she hits the ice, that goose is going to take off." Hahaha. I don't want to see people hurt, but if you are slipping on the ice in a parking lot what the heck do you expect to find on a trail?

The lesson of this hike was there are many reasons to turn around and call it a day. Never fail to heed the red flags. Play it safe and stay safe.

12 JENNINGS PEAK
Winter Hike

This mountain is really starting to tick me off. Our last attempt was a bust because of the impassable river crossing. I had made a big boo-boo by reading about Sandwich Dome in the guidebook and not Jennings Peak. If I had read about the latter, I would have discovered that you can cross the river by walking up the road for 0.1 mile and taking a small path that then reconnects to the main trail. CRAP! Oh well, with this new knowledge we made plans for a return attempt. Keith had strained a muscle shoveling snow, or watching TV, I cannot remember, so this hike would be Ian, Dave and myself. We rallied at Eastern Mountain Sports in Concord, stopped by our favorite bagel joint, then drove north. Most of the journey I had to endure Ian and Dave relentlessly picking on Keith, who was not there to defend himself. It created an ah-ha moment for me. Most of the time these clowns are harassing me about my rare, mild flatulence. It dawned on me that while I spent an entire day with the Pemigewasset SAR, and then another day with Fish and Game, I never once had a mishap. I now know it is constantly being picked on that upsets my delicate digestive system, resulting in the occasional toot. It really is THIER fault. I do know, however, that it is never cool to break wind in an elevator. That is wrong on so many levels.

The temperature had warmed a few days before, then dropped drastically. I am pretty sure this year will be one of the coldest ever recorded. The goons didn't bring their snowshoes because they were sure it would be a hard-packed surface. I had brought mine because my secretary had just returned from a ski trip and informed me that they had just received five inches of fresh snow. We arrived at the trailhead to discover we had to trudge through new snow that in some areas had drifted 12 inches deep. Dave and Ian were begging me to don my snowshoes. No way! I was not going to break trail for those two fatty heads. I just left them on my backpack and carried them the whole way. That showed them.

The weather was great with temps around 25° F and no wind. Somehow, Frick and Frack had managed to intentionally fall behind, leaving me to break trail by barebooting. I set a record pace and, before we knew it, we were at the "steep" section. Someone had taken a 25-foot section of the "Dawn Wall," covered it with ice, sprinkled a bit of snow on it and placed it right in the trail. Dave muscled his way up while slipping and sliding. I followed, taking time to repeatedly jam my feet in until my spikes were either on rock or thick ice. I am pretty sure I soiled myself over the prospect of falling. Ian watched my clumsy ascent while standing frozen like a statue. Dave and I asked him if he was coming, and he responded "Nope!" We assured him the trail was better after that section. He still said "Nope!" Dave and I took off for the summit with him leading at a pace fit only for trail runners on crack. Every time he leads, I have a mental conversation about the need to carry a gun. Bang! "Oh sorry, did you need that knee for hiking?"

As Dave and I headed back, we were faced with the ice wall from hell. I did not see how Dave descended because I was getting my phone out to film him and, the next thing I knew, he was at the bottom. I am pretty sure he levitated down by demonic power. I started down and, on my first step, my feet slid out from underneath me. Ever notice how fast your mind works when you are pretty sure you are dying. I had four separate conversations going on all at once. The first one was "Slow yourself down or you will hit speeds of over 100 mph." I grabbed for a tree, but body weight plus motion overpowered the strength of one arm. The next tree to shoot past was closer, but body weight plus acceleration overpowered the strength of both arms. At this time the second conversation began … "You are probably going to die or at best break things you need." This was followed by the third conversation: "You know you have a whippet poll in your hand that is designed for self-arresting?" Who has time for that? Back to the first conversation "Slow yourself down!" I saw another tree. However, Dave was trying to hide behind it with half his face peering out. He had a look of terror as he viewed an avalanche of snow and flesh, with spikes and pointed poles, coming at him like a freight train. His eyes were the size of pie plates, and his mouth was frozen open as if screaming, but no sound was emitted. One foot hit the tree while a hiking pole jabbed the tree at face level. Fourth conversation was "Dear God, I could have injured him and made him uglier than he already is." For those who say you cannot scream, poop and piss yourself at the same time, I have news — been there done that! I was headed for the last two trees that were side by side before the trail took a sharp left. I had to stop. Thankfully, I was going a little slower and both feet hit both trees and brought my antics to an end. I stood up quickly to convince Dave I had the whole thing under control, but my smell betrayed me. I know if Darlene had witnessed the escapade, she would have immediately doubled my life insurance. Covered in snow, I was no worse for wear.

Dave and I headed down fast to see if we could catch up with Ian. We found another steep area where the lad had butt-slid down about 20 feet. He is not a risk taker like I am and therefore should live a long, healthy life. We started meeting people hiking up the trail and asked them if they met Ian. They said they had. We asked if he had been crying. They said he had. You have to love hikers who, in a demented way, can jump right into your story.

As we got to the river crossing (the one we skipped by walking down the road) we noticed it had a solid snow bridge across it that everyone had been using. Everyone except Ian, that is. We got to the car, shared war stories and realized that Sandwich Dome had whooped us again. It is no longer on my bucket list — it is now war! I will defeat you, you damned, cursed mountain. I will defeat you!

On a side note, Dave has started getting gray hair. Lots of it.

13 THE GUNSTOCK LOOP
Winter Hike

The Belknap Mountains are a small mountain range in the Lakes Region of New Hampshire. You can earn the Belknap Range patch by hiking 12 peaks. They are

Mount Rowe (1,690 feet), Gunstock Mountain (2,250), Belknap Mountain (2,382), Mount Klem (2,001), Mount Mack (1,945), Mount Anna (1,670), Straightback Mountain (1,910), Mount Major (1,786), Piper Mountain (2,044), Whiteface Mountain (1,664), Rand Mountain (1,883) and Quarry Mountain (1,894).

You can also earn the Belknap Red Line patch by hiking all the peaks and including the 65.5 miles of trails.

After earning these patches, I had no desire to ever hike these peaks again. But as fate would have it, the goons and I started to rely on these smaller, more southerly peaks to stay in shape during winter weather. Mostly we would do what we refer to as the Gunstock loop. Starting with Gunstock, over to Belknap, then to Piper and out. This hike is about 5 miles and in winter months allows us to hike it at nighttime. I now do the loop around eight to 12 times a year. Gunstock gives 1,000 feet of elevation gain in 9/10 of a mile, equaling the difficulty of any 4,000-footer.

I had checked the weather on a Monday and saw that both Wednesday and Thursday were perfect for a night hike. Dave and Ian were a go for Wednesday. As chaplain for the Raymond Police Department, I was called to do oral boards for potential future officers that day. When I left the station in the afternoon, I was shocked to see it was snowing. Dave met me at my house. We hopped in my truck and headed out to meet Ian at the trailhead parking lot. There was now

1/2 inch of very slick snow on the roads. As we were navigating the back roads leading to the trailhead, the road pitched steeply downward for about 100 feet and ended with a stop sign at a "T" intersection. I applied the brakes and went into a slide. Dave's vision was frozen on a large pine tree across the road. I was more concerned about traffic, and thankfully there was none. I blew the stop sign as Dave was white knuckling it on my dashboard. As I slid into the intersection, I let off the brakes and gunned it causing the truck to miraculously turn 90 degrees. I drove on like nothing had happened. When I glanced over at Dave, he was white as a sheet, but smiling. I had never noticed before how much he is graying lately.

Scientists inform us our planet is 70 percent water. As water is evaporated by the sun it is lifted into the atmosphere. When temperatures get to 32°, the droplets crystallize. As these small ice crystals start joining together, they get heavy enough to fall. If they are driven by winds they collide and are sanded down smaller, making the snow denser. You have probably heard the saying, "Little snow, big snow. Big snow, little snow."

Usually smaller snowflakes will produce deeper, more dense snow and larger flakes produce the lighter, fluffier snow. I have heard it said that there are no two snowflakes the same, and that people are like snowflakes. I agree. The goons I hike with are cold-hearted, as dense as "little snow" and make hiking difficult. (We get a lot of flakes in New Hampshire; most of them are out-of-staters.)

The snow we experienced on this hike was the light, puffy kind.

On our ascent, the snow was about 3/4 of an inch deep. Underneath the snow, the trail was solid ice, affording us great traction with our spikes. I was in the lead, setting a pace that was grueling for Dave and Ian and they kept falling behind. I love hiking while it is snowing. Don't know why. Just do. I think it started as a kid when I could go into the woods behind my house without having to drive in the stuff. After summiting Gunstock, the snow was really coming down. We resorted to our headlamps and headed off to Belknap, then over to Piper. We had been at it for under two hours as we started descending the Piper Trail, and then things started getting interesting. By now there was three inches of snow covering sheer ice. With each step, your body weight compresses the snow to 7/8ths. Our spikes are 5/8ths. Doing the math, you can see that the snow depth was just enough to make our spikes ineffective as we made our way down a trail of steep ice. I started noticing I was slipping quite a bit and the whole adventure was becoming treacherous. My son had told me about a phenomenon known as an "expert halo." As a member of an SAR team, he said that sometimes the more experienced a hiker becomes, the easier it is to not pay attention to red flags. In the SAR community, rescuers can take risks that can create an IWI, an incident within an incident, where rescuers now need rescuing. I do not consider myself an expert and in our defense these three inches were never forecasted.

Though we slowed our descent, all three of us were slipping and sliding. Ian had a wipeout and did a short butt slide. It dawned on me that the size of a mountain means nothing, a fall resulting in a broken limb can happen on level ground. We were grateful to make it out of there with no issues. Conditions can change fast, so you have to heed those red flags. No expert halo for Ian or me, and Dave never lost his horns. The thought of a halo on Dave? Please, be real!

14 Fourth Overnighter

Ian and Dave had been pestering me for weeks to do another overnighter. Since I first turned them on to the experience, they could not get enough and had devolved into a couple of 5-year-olds whining for candy. This time the weather forecast was perfect, and I selected a location that would reward us with both a sunset and sunrise. I was as happy as a constipated man who just found a half gallon of prune juice.

We stopped at a Subway and bought dinner, then drove due north into the Whites. Arriving at the trailhead, we hoisted our packs and began the journey. It was a superb autumn day, rich with the colors and smells of the fall foliage. There are three levels of foliage enjoyment. First, Googling pictures of fall in New England, Second, visiting New Hampshire in mid-October, Third, camping out in the center of God's artistic palate of color. When we reached our destination, we found ourselves in the center of an ocean filled with red, yellow, orange and maroon crowned with brilliant blue sky. We slid off our packs and they lay where they fell as we bounced from spot to spot, gazing in wonder in every direction. Each degree the sun set lit whole mountain ranges in ever-changing variations of dynamic beauty. It was the best foliage I had ever seen.

A small group of people who were there left as the sun was fading. We started our search for the perfect place to lay out our sleeping bags. The wind had picked up, so we located an area that was shielded from the wind, set out our sleep systems, and ate dinner. Somehow all the trash ended up in my pack. These guys just do not know how not to be jerks. We lay awake in our sleeping bags talking about everything imaginable until talk was overpowered by sleep. At 11 p.m., I awoke to relieve myself, maxed the volume on my phone and loudly sang along to Lord Huron's "I Ain't Dead Yet." Put trash in my pack, will ya! The goons woke up, grumbled, then laughed, then fell silent as the events of the day, combined with the cool, fresh mountain air caused us to succumb to our weariness.

We awoke well before sunrise. When I say "we" I mean "me," but I woke the goons up because they looked too comfortable and that is not what camping is about. When it is brisk out, it is hard to leave the warmth of a sleeping bag, especially when it is still dark out. They tried to go back to sleep, but my rapid-fire jokes, mixed in with a song or two, were more than they could withstand. Not only that, but I had gotten up and was starting to make breakfast and they were concerned I might be eating their food. (Like I would ever do something like that.) I may have also accidentally shone my headlamp in their eyes as I was cooking my delicious Mountain House *Egg Scrambler* breakfast. Soon they were crawling out of their sleeping bags like distempered bears after hibernation. We ate breakfast while laughing and chatting like school children — well, I was laughing and chatting, they were grunting and cursing about something. How their wives put up with them is an enigma. As the light of day dawned over the first range, with coffee in hand, we witnessed its glorious arrival. After taking hundreds of pictures, the guys had finally sobered up from their grogginess, thanked me profusely, and offered to buy me coffee on the ride home. I usually do not accept this kind of gratuity because I do what I do out of the kindness of who I am. It just comes naturally.

Packing up gear after an overnighter does not go quite as well as when first packing it in the comfort of your home. It becomes more of a "stuff it all in as fast as you can," you can sort it out later. The weather was clouding up a bit as we hit the trail out. More people had arrived to enjoy the sunrise, signaling to us it was time to go. On the hike out, we reminisced about the experience and started making plans for the next adventure. I cannot remember exactly, but I think while humming a song or two I heard Dave ask Ian "Should we bring him?"

15 Fifth Overnighter

Ian had been doing some research for an overnight stay in a remote shelter before he floated the idea by me and Dave. The plan was to park at the Arethusa-Ripley Trail parking lot off Route 302 and take the Ethan Pond Trail for about 2.5 miles to the Ethan Pond Shelter. The next morning, we would hike the rest of the Ethan Pond Trail and connect to the Zealand Trail heading out to a car we had previously dropped off, making the entire trip about 9.5 miles. The elevation gain would only be about 1,700 feet to the shelter. After that, it was mostly flat hiking through the Zealand Notch. It sounded like a sweet deal. Being a Friday, I had to wait for Dave and Ian to get off work, change into their hiking gear, meet up and head out. The game plan was to meet up with Ian at the Zealand Road parking lot where we would leave Dave's car, then drive to the trailhead.

We knew we would be hiking in the dark. The weather forecast was calling for a damp drizzle overnight and clearing in the morning. Because it was late October and there was the lousy weather, we knew we would have the shelter to ourselves.

We arrived on schedule to find the last car leaving the parking lot. We shouldered our packs, put on our headlamps, and started into the woods pumped about the idea of having a deep-woods shelter all to ourselves. It was a little cool with lots of fog. As we hiked in, I noticed lone footprints on some of the rocks. I said, "Hey guys, I think that car dropped off a hiker, so I don't think we will have the shelter all to ourselves." It was no big deal as the shelter slept six to eight people. The 2.5 miles takes a lot longer to hike in the dark and I thought the trail would never end. We turned right on a side path leading to the shelter and had to do some minor rock hopping by Ethan Pond. Arriving at the shelter we found it full. YOU HAVE TO BE @#^#$ KIDDING ME! Where, what, how??? I was speechless. You could not have surprised me more if Epstein actually committed suicide. The selfish slobs in the cabin were younger and had no consideration for their elders. One of them poked his head out of his sleeping bag, pointed and said, "The tent shelters are over there." Well, guess what, Einstein? WE DIDN'T BRING TENTS! We never suspected in a million years that there would be other half-crazed people who would hike in a heavy drizzle to sleep in a shelter. What is the word coming to? We muttered a conversation between the three of us as to whether we thought we could kick their butts. Being a man of non-violence, I headed to the tent platforms.

Tent platforms are 10x10 decks with some loops around the edges where you can lash a tent. They were already damp from the moisture-laden fog. My normally jovial mood was going down in flames. It was late, we were tired, and there were no other options. We set out our sleeping bags and air pads, crawled in and prayed the weather didn't worsen. At one point in the middle of the night I woke to use the facilities, which basically meant standing at the edge of the platform and letting it rip. While doing my thing I tried to look around the woods. The heavy drizzle was going sideways across the beam of my headlamp. I could not even see 20 feet into the woods. Everything was getting wet and the wind had picked up substantially. I crawled back into my bag and willed myself to sleep.

I was awakened by Dave, who was up and packing. Ian was just starting to wake. Dave did not want breakfast, he just wanted to start moving. That ain't gonna happen. I fired up my stove and heated up some breakfast and coffee, as did Ian. Mr. Morning had put on his pack and went to be one with nature by the pond. Ian and I ate, packed up our wet gear and went to meet Dave. The stars were fading as the sky was just starting to lighten. I must admit the view at the pond was peaceful.

We connected back with the Ethan Pond Trail and started the seven-mile hike out. One of the things that amazed me is how wet and muddy some of the forests are, even at elevation. It was so wet there were unusually long spans of bog bridges. Bog bridges are usually two 3 x 6's, side by side with a two-inch gap between them and supporting 6 x 6's at either end. They are anywhere from 8 to 12 feet long and over the years they sink a little, making them pitch. Because air can flow underneath them, they can freeze faster than the ground. After our night of drizzle, the temps had dropped and these bog bridges were covered with a thin layer of ice. This hike was fast becoming a nightmare. To slip off a bridge would mean sinking up to your armpits in swamp, making the pace slow and tenuous.

My son had bought me an awesome filter system called a Salomon soft flask. I stopped along the North Fork and replenished all my Nalgene bottles. Just because you are soaking wet on the outside does not mean you do not need to stay hydrated on the inside.

The clouds were breaking up, which allowed the sun to peek through from time to time, drying us off and warming us. The elevation increased just enough, allowing us to leave the bog bridges behind. I had never experienced a trail with so many crazy bog bridges. As we headed into the notch, the trail became like something you would see in *Hiking Digest Magazine* and the views were suddenly spectacular. Our fortune was turning and the hike was now enjoyable. There is one section of trail where the cliffs rose above you on the right side and dropped below you on the left side with only the narrow width of the trail to walk on. To our amazement a moose had gone before us, leaving its deep tracks in the dirt. Hard to imagine such a large animal on such a singular trail as this.

After having a fitful night of unrestful sleep, navigating icy bog bridges, and hiking these last seven miles, we were weary, but strangely happy. Not all plans go as expected. You must be prepared and be willing to adapt, improvise and overcome. If you are ever inclined to venture out and spend a night in a shelter ... bring a tent!!!

16 The Hike of a Lifetime

Dave and I had been talking about the possibility of putting together a 30- to 45-minute presentation that would marry the components of hiking with living life. We wanted to make it appealing to hikers and non-hikers alike. After some months of preparation, it all came together. We selected photos we had taken on all the stages of a hike and produced a beautiful PowerPoint presentation. The overall theme is that hiking is not just about the summits or the views. It involves planning, packing, traveling, hiking in all conditions, leaving no trace, summits, hiking out, photos, friendships, cleaning and repairing gear, and planning for the next hike.

Life is like that. It is not just about the big events like getting a driver's license, continuing education, career, marriage, family or retirement. Life is the whole journey. Learning to enjoy and value the good, bad and the ugly. Sometimes the sun is shining and life is great, other times the weather is foul, but you still have to stay the course. The presentation was ready.

We decided Dave would introduce each stage of hiking and I would talk about how it mirrors the journey of life. We had our first opportunity with the Raymond Rotary Club. The presentation went great. We fine-tuned it and were invited to two more Rotary Clubs, a private high school, and a large group of business professionals. Each event was appreciated and warmly received. One Rotary Club said it was the best presentation they had ever had. Dave and I enjoyed each opportunity.

If you know of a venue that would be interested in a family-fun presentation about the similarities of hiking and living life, let us know. Hopefully more people will realize life is a gift and every part of the journey is to be welcomed, learned from and enjoyed. We would love nothing more than to know everyone is on the hike of a lifetime.

17 Winter Solo Overnighter

When I was pondering the content of this book, I decided on the combination of winter hiking, solo hiking and overnighters. Then, like a flash from midlife crisis, the thought came of attempting a solo winter overnighter, ending the book with a bang. I know what you are thinking, "Ken, don't do it!" Or "Ken, that is way too dangerous!" I know, right. But the real story is even worse. It is a nail-biting, page turner, so without further ado ...

Winter hiking is more dangerous than any other time of year. The risks are greater. Personally, I hate winter hiking. Too much slipping and sliding, heavier packs, below-zero temps. The whole thing is bothersome. Likewise, solo hiking is chancier than going with others. If there is an accident or injury, you have no one to rely on. Unless you hike with the goons I hike with, in that case you may be better off on your own rather than relying on Moe, Larry and Curly. Camping alone is a lot scarier because my imagination is uncontrollable and takes my thoughts into places they should not go. On the upside, when camping out with Dave, Ian and Keith, if a wild animal attacked, there is a 75 percent I would be OK. I still maintain a wild animal would probably desire my succulent sweetness compared to their putrid, smelly, disease-ridden flesh, so my calculations may be way off.

This winter was stupid-cold. It finally got to where I was internally, constantly cold. Even in my house with a hoodie on, my hands and feet would feel cold. I remember my dear, sweet mom always saying her feet felt like two blocks of ice. At 63, I was beginning to understand her plight. Usually every January we would have a week of single-digit temps. This year it started in December and did not let up until mid-March. After so many sub-zero hikes, it was catching up to me. I do not own extreme winter gear. The stuff I own will suffice, but it is not the greatest. My idea of the right gear would include a hotel room with hot tub, large-screen TV and free breakfast.

I was waiting patiently for a night when the temps would be in the high 30's, but the weeks were flying by. Finally, the last week of winter warmed up and a window opened up that would be my last chance for the planned overnighter. I had been looking at spending a night in Pawtuckaway State Park. The snow was, for the most part, gone. I could hike in a couple of miles and camp out without needing a tent. I know some of you are thinking, "Really? That's it?" Yes, that is it. One real sportsman-like gentleman told me of a shelter, halfway up Mount Washington, that would be perfect. "In fact," he said, "you sometimes have to dig your way into it through deep snow." No! Nada. Nope. Nein. NEVER!

After sharing my plans with Dave, he immediately started busting my bubble, complaining the location would not count because it was not far enough north, nor on a mountain. I reminded him it was to be a solo winter overnighter, there were no other qualifiers. He relentlessly shamed me into changing my plans. He was peskier than a dog humping a person's leg. I gave in. I would travel north where there was still 12 inches of snow on the ground, hike a mountain and spend the night.

Eleanor Roosevelt once said, "No one can make you feel anything you do not choose to feel." This will be the last time I ever let someone shame me into anything. The dirt road in was a mud fest. Within two days after my hike, they actually closed the road down. I arrived at the trial head at 4:10 p.m., shouldered an unbelievably heavy pack and started up. The conditions were ridiculous. At 40° F, the snow was sloppy. In the hiking world, conditions like this are referred to as "mashed potatoes." Even with spikes, the traction was horrible. It is the kind of hiking that fatigues you quickly. When solo hiking, you are left alone to your own thoughts. You need to be OK with that. My thoughts were turning dark towards Dave for bullying me into this horrible predicament. The farther I hiked, the more my internal dialogue soured. The melting runoff was creating small streams under the snow that were undetectable until you postholed through a weakened snow bridge and strained a knee. I am pretty sure your knees should not sound like nuts and bolts in a blender. The steeper the trail became, the more I was slipping under the load of my overnight gear. When I thought it could get no worse, I began to encounter ice flows like you would find on Everest. I was sweating heavily and wondering if I could manage the night alone in the deep forest. Just before conceding defeat, I came across a small cabin. Wow, I had never seen it before on previous hikes, yet there it was. At first, I thought it was a mirage from delirium. As I investigated, I was delighted to realize that the small porch was roofed. Just then it began raining. "No way," I thought. I had decided to leave my heavy tent behind because four of the five weather sites I had looked at called for a clear night and the fifth said only a 10 percent chance of rain. As I rested on the porch, the rain continued. In fact, it rained for the next 45 minutes. I started liking the porch. It was dry. I took a picture and texted it to the guys. The pushback was immediate. "That's not camping" was the accusation. I replied it was no different than a shelter. In fact, a shelter would have more sides. I really did not care what my tormentors thought. The sun was setting, it was raining, and God had provided me a dry location. By the way, if any of the goons tell you a tall tale other than the facts I share, it is fake news, plain and simple. They get jealous when they see how God provides for me.

I got my gear out and set up for the night. One of the things I started realizing about winter overnighters was that it would be dark at 5 p.m. and not get light until 7 a.m. That's a long time to stay in a sleeping bag! I boiled water in my Jetboil and heated a Mountain House meal of chicken with dumplings. The warm food was comforting as the night began to get cooler. I put on some dry clothing and slid into my sleeping bag. That was when I heard it: a crunch. A little later, crunch, crunch, crunch. A short time after that, crunch, crunch, CRUNCH! And there he was... Captain Crunch. Hahaha. Darlene tells me to grow up, but it ain't gonna happen.

The first time I awoke for a nature call, I lay still in the dark and listened. I know people insist there are no wolves or mountain lions in New Hampshire, but my imagination can hear them, see them, even smell them. Some people reported they have seen them. I read about it on the Internet. Even if not in our state, I could easily picture a distempered, non-hibernating bear or even Bigfoot. Anyway, a guy has to put that foolishness aside, relieve himself, then move like lightning back into the warm safety of his sleeping bag. I never said I was not chicken. Once, while hiking, I saw a bear that turned out to be stump, then a moose that turned out to be a blowdown, then a pair of hideous alien creatures that turned out to be Ian and Keith. The next time I awakened, I was greeted by a full moonlit night with stars everywhere. The moonlight on the snow made my lamp unnecessary. On the downside, I still had four hours before morning and had developed a slight headache. I took a couple of Tylenol and turned in again.

I woke up an hour before sunrise to find I was soaking wet from sweat. I believe I may have had a cold, but I sweated it out. I took off my base layer shirt and put on my mid-layer puffy jacket. I decided to get up and make breakfast and coffee, not from hunger, but more out of boredom. The warm food and drink really helped. I listened to some music and waited for what became a slow, soft sunrise.

Though I spent 10 hours in my sleeping bag, I did not feel completely refreshed. That is to be expected on an overnighter. The sun finally made a spectacular appearance, and I was rewarded with some prime pictures. My thoughts were to head out and skip the summit. I decided to finish the hike. I am glad I did as it turned out to be an awesome finish to a tough overnighter. The summit was amazing and I never saw another hiker throughout the entire ordeal. Dave, Ian and Keith were all amazed at my self-determination to accomplish such an incredible goal, but for me it was just another day of hiking. After all, it was for the book.

18 Eveready Bunny vs. Roadkill

Ever notice on some hikes you start out strong only to find your legs are soon shot and energy has evaporated like a drop of water on a hot skillet? I am not talking about the constant need to recover breathing and heart rates. I am talking about the old legs not agreeing to go hiking. You are pushing up a mountain, doing pretty well, when all of the sudden your legs say "Yeah, you know what? I am really not doing this today. Have fun without me."

It was early April and rainy, yet one Saturday turned for the good with the promise of sunshine, but high winds. Ian contacted the group, wanting to hike. Keith was still out with an injury and Dave was out with bursitis, so I was the dope who said, "I'll go, I'll go." We decided to do a two-car drop in order to complete Gunstock, Belknap, Piper and Swett. Gunstock is a killer, gaining 1,000 feet of elevation fast. A third of the way up, my legs start giving me attitude. I was exhausted, fatigued, worn out, tired and just plain pooped. I do not know why that happens. Some days you feel invincible, like the *Energizer Bunny*, and other days you feel like roadkill. We stopped and I had a snack and rested. When we resumed, I noticed Ian was wearing every stitch of clothing he had brought because I was moving so slow that he started freezing up. Every step was torture. I kept focusing on the next step, then the next one. We stopped again. And again. What was wrong with me? I began to wonder if there was a serious medical condition that I was unaware of like cancer, or a heart blockage, or an internal parasite that was eating away at my leg muscles. Ian asked me to be quiet as I was eating away at his nerves. When we made it to the summit of Gunstock, I was done. My tank was out of gas. Ian made a comment about that being the worst of it and everything was easy from here on out. Hahaha. As I contemplated how long it would take his body to decompose in the woods, we started descending and my legs seemed OK with that. We hit ice going up Belknap and resorted to our spikes.

Dang, I usually do this loop nonstop, but I had to stop multiple times. It was embarrassing. How do you cure muscle-eating parasites? We met a few hikers here and there, but I noticed when I would try to say hello, what came out was more like a cough from a donkey with asthma. We crossed Belknap and headed down the other side, again deceiving my legs for a little while. While descending we met this young girl coming up, taking long powerful strides without effort. She was even smiling. I cannot stand people like that, showing off in front of a handicapped hiker. What is wrong with people? We headed up Piper. Oh my God! Someone please shoot me. That is what they do to lame horses and it would be fine with me. Usually we do the loop in 2.5 hours. It was now 3 hours into the hike and we were just heading up Piper. We stopped. Again! We ate more, hydrated and rested. We were also putting on and taking off our spikes quite a bit because of the April trail conditions. As we headed across the Piper ridge, I was reminded of how much I love that section of trail. My legs were now in a coma with no signals coming in. They were toast!

Was it winter fatigue? Was it me trying to lose weight and not being fueled up enough? Was it because I had done nothing in the way of physical activity for a week? Was it Ian driving me like Pharaoh building the pyramids? Lack of hydration? Full moon? Aliens?

I told Ian I was going to pass on Mount Swett. There is a lot of elevation drop on the way to Swett that I would have to make up coming back out and I just could not do it. We passed the trail heading to Swett and I cried a tear of joy. As we trudged on, Ian said "You wanna do Mount Whiteface?" Whiteface is a two-mile out-and-back, but it does not have huge elevation. He quickly added more enticement by saying "Come on, what else were you going to do today anyway?" Well, I had been thinking of lying on my couch and not moving for the next three days but there was something tempting about the proposition. The next thing I knew I had crossed the stone wall that put us on the trail to Whiteface.

Why do we do stupid things? Play stupid games, win stupid prizes. You would think that after six years of hiking everything in New Hampshire that I would know better. I guess my legs were so tired that the pain made my mind go brain-dead. We met more hikers as we made our way out of the woods who looked like they were having fun.

I detested each one of them. I have no excuses for the pitiful performance, only questions. Why was that hike so miserable? I should have been able to do that non-stop any day of the week. My only satisfactory answer ... some days you are roadkill.

19 TENTS

Just bought another tent. Yup, that makes five. I never inform Darlene of my purchases. She thinks she buys me all my gear at Christmas and birthdays. What the woman does not know won't hurt her and if she ever finds out it will help me stay in shape as I run for my life. As they say, "Conflict is the spice of marriage."

Hiking is a way of life and hiking equipment is a way of staying poor. There is seemingly sound wisdom behind every purchase, yet buyer's remorse is usually soon to follow. On the upside, I think I am at the place where I can start guided tours and outfit up to 20 people.

Tent No. 1 is a Hillary dome tent, large enough for three people, gear and a dog. It is really designed for car camping. It weighs about 900 pounds and is so large you need the car to carry it. It does have a cool logo commemorating the 1953 expedition of Sir Edmund Hillary, first person to climb Mount Everest, not counting Zeg Sook in 6,231 B.C.

Tent No. 2 is an Alps Mountaineering Zephyr 2 backpacking tent. This is the infamous tent that accompanied me on my trip over the three Bonds. It is a great tent, but like many of the older tents, it weighs six to seven pounds. Unthinkable in today's standards. You cannot be stupid-light with a six-pound tent. Still, I really like the tent and was able to shave its packed weight to about five pounds.

Tent No. 3 is not really a tent. It is a Sea to Summit Pyramid Net. It is basically a one-person mosquito net that weighs only 8.6 ounces. It seemed a practical purchase for an overnighter that promises clear weather, keeping you from dying of exsanguination.

Tent No. 4 is a River Country Products Pole tent. This was a compulsive purchase. I saw it on Amazon, it was lightweight at only three pounds, it had plenty of room and, most importantly, it was green. Green being my favorite color, that was the tipping point. I shopped for two years to find and buy a green pickup truck. Who does that?

A pole tent is light because it uses your hiking poles for the support. Unfortunately, my Black Diamond poles are not adjustable so I will have to remove the snow baskets from my winter poles and use them. Life ... it takes all my time. This tent is also a single wall tent, which I understand can build condensation. I have yet to sleep out in this tent. But I plan to do so soon. I have to. It's green!!!

Tent No. 5, and the last tent I will ever buy, is a Big Agnes Tiger Wall Ultralight two-person, solution-dyed tent with mtnGLO LED light system built in. Drop the mic, the curtain falls, everyone go home. Dang! How could I resist? This thing only weighs 2.8 pounds. Crazy. Large enough for me and my gear — and with its own lights. All the seams are taped and sealed, it packs small and has its own lights. I am fine with the color, yellow, and the rainfly offers plenty of dry space outside the tent and IT HAS ITS OWN FREAKING LIGHTS!!!

Although I have not yet used my Big Agnus, I know it was a wise purchase.

So, yeah, five tents.

20 THE TALE OF TWO CLIMATES
Solo Hike

New Hampshire is by far the most beautiful place in New England. Heck, in the country. Maybe the world. Dare I say the UNIVERSE! There I said it. When I talk about its beauty I am talking about its natural beauty. The seacoast, the lakes, the White Mountains, its vast areas of protected wilderness and, of course, its climate and seasons. You can keep Manchester.

The reason this became a solo hike starts with Dave. Dave reminds me of Nancy Pelosi: both are as ugly as sin, had enough shots and boosters to make them scientific cocktail experiments, and still ended up with Covid. That took him out of the rotation for hiking. I had spent three hours with Dave just prior to his symptoms manifesting. Even though my natural rugged immunity, strength and good looks killed the virus on contact, Keith wanted nothing to do with me. He was out of the lineup. Ian had to work, leaving me with one option: a solo hike.

Finally, I was free from the Three Amigos and could enjoy nature at my pace. My grin turned into a smile, then a laugh, then full diabolical hysteria. Darlene said, "Stop jumping up and down. Are you crazy or something?" Yeah, crazy. Hehehe. Now what to hike?

For some reason I had recently struggled on Gunstock at 2,244 feet, so I decided on North Kinsman at 4,274 because I am a dope. The weather was looking perfect — sunny, hardly any wind, and 37° F on the summit. Trail condition reports said two feet of snow on the summit and snowshoes may be needed. I could have hiked something smaller that would not have had any snow, but no. I packed my full winter kit. Extra clothes, snacks, spikes, snowshoes, whippet pole, extra hydration, medical and repair equipment — the works. When I picked up my pack, I almost threw my back out. Holy smokes, that was heavy. At least I was not doing the five-mile Gunstock loop. This hike would only be eight miles. What a dope.

On the drive up, I got a Dunkin' blueberry coffee with an egg, sausage and cheese on a cinnamon-raisin bagel — the stuff that tamed the wild frontier. When arriving at the parking lot, there was only one other car there. This would be a real solo with plenty of solitude. My approach was from the west side via the Mount Kinsman Trail. I had done the Fishin' Jimmy trail on the east side once and once was enough. With youthful enthusiasm, I lifted my pack, almost giving myself a hernia, grabbed my poles and headed up. At the trail sign, someone had found and left a Nalgene bottle. What kind of dope loses stuff on a hike?

The first section of the trail was a gentle path through a pine forest, the fallen pine needles making a soft, quiet hike. This allowed both legs and mind a warmup time for what lay ahead. Deep in thought, I was meditating on whether I would make it out alive. Within the first half hour, a song from the 1960's came into my mind and it would be my torturer for the rest of the hike. I do not know why that happens, but it seems to be one of the downsides of solo hiking.

The sun was shining, the trail was beautiful, and I was happy to be out.

The path turned into a Jeep trail covered in round, ankle-twisting rocks, with slightly more elevation gain, and water flowing down it. After some time, it did not feel right. Though I had a paper map with me, I had forgotten to load the AllTrails map on my phone. I noticed I had a good signal, so I stopped and loaded it. It revealed that I was where I needed to be. At two miles in, there were three small river crossings, then the ice started. I put my spikes on. Within the next mile everything changed from a warm, snowless, fall-like hike to a winter wonderland with two feet of snowpack and the trees covered in an inch of fresh fallen snow. The air was cooler, invigorating, as I went from one climate to a completely different one in moments. The elevation was now much more rigorous. I met the other hiker from the car in the parking lot as he was coming down. He informed me I did not need snowshoes. Although I did not like the extra weight, I would rather have them and not need them than need them and not have them, especially on a solo hike.

The views at the summit were incredible. Cannon, Lafayette, Lincoln, Liberty and Flume were snow-covered and shining in the bright golden sunshine, making them more glorious than usual. It was epic. I took loads of pics, hydrated and started making my way down. The time at the summit had chilled my hands, so I retrieved my EMS mitts from my pack. It pays to pack.

Being solo meant there was no rush. I took pictures of waterfalls, snow-covered trees in the sunlight, the trail stretching out in front of me — just about everything. I captured the extreme change between the conditions at the base versus the summit. I do not ever remember a hike where the contrast was so stark. The hike had thrown everything at me. Dry trail, rocks, mud, wet rocks, rivers, ice, snow, frozen snow-covered trees, back to mud and moss-covered rocks with temps at the base in the 60's. I had made good time on the snow and ice but slowed considerably on rocks and roots.

I met a guy as he headed up, then a woman, later another guy with his dog, then I met an older gentleman named Peter. I stepped off trail to let him go past. Trail etiquette says those going down stop for those going up. Rather than just a polite, "Hello," then continuing, he stopped, and we spent the next 20 minutes in delightful conversation. Peter lives close by so he hikes North Kinsman weekly to stay in shape. He used to belong to SAR when younger, then he worked for AMC (Appalachian Mountain Club). He used to be a journalist but has since retired. Somehow he found out that I authored two books, (available on Amazon) and was now working on a third. I love meeting super-friendly hikers like Peter. He added to the experience of the hike.

After my visit with Peter, I noticed my legs did not want to cooperate for the remainder of the hike. They had solidified into non-bending appendages in quite a bit of pain. I stopped to remove my spikes and pack them away. I also wanted to pack my mitts that I had jammed into my pants pockets. To my surprise, I had lost a mitten. Who loses stuff on a hike? Me, that's who! What a dope.

This hike turned out to be the definition of a non-winter winter hike. It was amazing.

BDE.

21 Hair of the Dog

Sometimes when people wake up with a pounding hangover, someone will offer them another drink while making the comment, "A hair of the dog that bit you." I never understood how drinking more could possibly make you feel better when you are bowl yodeling and doing the liquid laugh, as your head feels like it is going to explode. I also never understood the statement about the "hair of the dog."

Digging into some history I found that the phrase comes from an old English belief that when someone was bitten by a rabid dog, one could, supposedly, make a potion from one of the dog's hairs and place it into the wound, preventing the victim from getting rabies. I do not think that belief stood the test of medical science. Over time the saying came to mean have another go at whatever it was that knocked you down.

For me it has always meant Mount Waumbek. Five years ago, it was the first 4,000-footer I attempted while 55 pounds overweight and completely unconditioned. The full story is in my first book but, suffice it to say I could not walk for the next five days. Keith accompanied me and still reminds me of, when out of nowhere, the sky opened up with a drenching rain and I, being unable to continue, sat on a rock in the middle of the trail, defeated, discouraged and in excruciating pain. He said, "You looked like a drowned rat." After surviving hiking for the last five years, I had always wanted another go at Waumbek.

The day came in April 2022, when Keith was attempting his "Over 70" list of the 48 4,000 footers. He had faithfully hiked with me as I was doing my list, so I figured it was only right to return the favor. Ian joined us and we drove far north to the trailhead.

Although this hike is neither a solo, winter or overnighter, I am including the story because, for me, it is coming full circle. Now a seasoned, experienced hiker, I stood facing Waumbek, looking for a "hair of the dog that bit me."

The day was sunny, yet cool. It would later warm up to 62 but the early morning was still chilly. As we headed up, we ran into what you would expect on an April hike: water, mud, flowing water and slippery rocks. I took it all in stride. My hope was to go non-stop to the summit. I had hiked North Kinsman on Monday. On Tuesday I hiked 5.5 miles in Pawtuckaway State Park. On Wednesday afternoon I hiked the 5.5-mile Gunstock loop, and now, on Friday, Mount Waumbek. We stopped to delayer after a mile, then stopped again after another mile to put on our spikes as ice appeared. We actually stopped a number of times before summiting. I realized a couple of things on this hike. Stopping regularly for 60 seconds to recover your heart and breathing rates is better than pushing so hard you have to stop for 5 to 10 minutes. That habit had been developed by experience. The second thing I realized is that a 4,000-foot mountain is still a 4,000-foot mountain. It is a push. I began to realize it was OK for this mountain to have kicked my butt. It is a long 3.7 miles to the summit. I had felt like an out-of-shape failure, but now, being conditioned, I realized, these mountains are big and they exact their pound of flesh from most hikers. I have seen the 20-year-old trail runners. Good for them. I have also witnessed out-of-shape folks, children and older hikers pushing hard and earning the right to feel proud of their accomplishment of summiting. I even met a gal on this hike who told me she cried three times the first time she hiked a 4,000-footer. Hats off to every one of them. For whatever reason you hike or whatever shape you are in, the mountains are a gift.

The next time you hike a mountain that taxes you to the limit, get some rest, do some stretching, get your maps to pick the next hike and have a "hair of the dog that bit you". You may never get rabies, but people will think you are crazy.

22 Why Do You Hike?

Only in New Hampshire would the thought of packing spikes and bug spray even make sense. After a cold start in May, the weather finally turned. Though higher elevations were still getting sporadic snow, the lower elevation was in bloom and the bugs were starting to make their appearance. Repellant and spikes, what a combo.

Originally, I was going to do a solo hike, but Ian was just recuperating from Covid and had been going stir-crazy from being house bound. I felt horrible for the lad, so I invited him to join me. He was all-in. Dave was on a plane heading to Colorado to see his son and Keith had gone fishing. Ian agreed to meet me at the trailhead of Welch Mountain/Dickey Mountain at 7 a.m. The loop over both peaks is 4.4 miles, gaining 1,800 feet of elevation. That may not seem much, but this trail has it all — steep slab rock, technical formations, scrambles and incredible views.

My hope was to ask every person I met why they hiked. The problem was that Ian and I were the first in the parking lot and, heading out on the customary counterclockwise direction, I figured we would not run into other hikers.

The conditions were perfect: sunny, mild breeze, 60° F. Though the trail was muddy, the snow and ice were gone. After a short time, we came to the first outlook. Ian commented that it was little work for the great views. I chuckled because I knew what lay ahead. After that first stop, the trail gets insanely steep. Having never done this hike, Ian was wrestling with the difficulty of some of the scrambles. At one point he said, "If you didn't want to be my friend you could have just texted me." Hahaha, like I would do something like this on purpose. Who does he think I am? Dave? The guidebook says, "The open ledges are grippy when dry, but use caution if wet." In a number of places, water was running down the slab rock. In one of the steepest areas, while on all fours, I slipped down about three inches. I don't know what was worse — crapping my pants or seeing my life flash before my eyes. By now Ian was hyperventilating and I kept lying. "That's the last of the tough spots," I told him. Sure this trail gives you cause to pucker, but isn't that why we hike? To feel alive?

We did the scrambles and the steep portions and made it to the summit. I showed Ian where I had lost my L.L. Bean Nalgene bottle years before, then we headed down Welch and over to Dickey Mountain. More wet, steep, slab rock. I love this trail. Just before reaching the ledges, we ran into two guys coming up in a clockwise direction. Here was my chance. I retrieved my pen and pad, asked them their names and why they hiked?

These guys were the real deal. They live locally and hike Welch-Dickey weekly. Ned, who lives in Campton N.H., said he hikes in the spring to get conditioned. At 70, he said it helps him feel young and exhilarated. "Hiking is still a thrill," he added. His favorite hike is Mount Zealand to the three Bonds and out again, which is about 20 miles. Charlie, who is from Ashland, N.H., said he loves the views and feels alive when in nature. He said, "It energizes me." I think they will need that energy as they are both working on redlining all the trails in the Presidential Range. Just then a trail runner ran past us. What the ... how!?

We said our goodbyes and Ian and I headed down. Ian made an astute observation that there are not many 4.4-mile trails that, when completed, make you feel like you did a much longer hike. Welch-Dickey sure is one of those. In fact, it is becoming one of my favorites.

Arriving at the parking lot, we found it a beehive of activity. Ian drove off and I got pad and pen and started the interviews.

Sue, from New Hampton, N.H., and Patty, from Holderness, N.H., were trying to corral their three dogs, Lenny, Carlos, and Eddie, when I approached them. They hike to let their dogs run and have fun, as well as to share their friendship and escape the crazies of society. They try to get out a couple of times a week.

Matt, from Nashua, NH, says he hikes to get in better shape and he enjoys everything about it. Adam, also from Nashua, says it is all about the peace and quiet. They said they have lots of other hobbies as well, such as kayaking, so they don't get out to hike as much as they would like.

Ned and Janet were from Connecticut. They don't get to New Hampshire often, but they were here training for a September assault on Mount Washington. They said they hike for the fun of it.

Liz, from Manchester, N.H., said her online job involves lots of phone calls, making hiking a way to escape. She loves the accomplishment of hiking, especially solo hiking in winter.

When Krista, who is from Barre, Mass., heard that I had lost a lot of weight hiking, this thin, fit woman told me she had lost 300 pounds. Dear mother, that is two whole other people. She loves hiking because nature is calming (not the wet slab rock!!!). She finds it relaxing and extremely good for the soul. Justin, from Clinton, Mass., says he likes the adventure of bushwhacking. He is good at navigating and sometimes tries to get lost to work his way back to the trail.

To all my new friends I would say, rock on. You are part of why I hike. There are a lot of awesome folks out on the trail. For some reason, all these fine folks said they would buy my book. How did they know? I was stunned. How did they figure it out? Oh yeah, it was because I wrote my name down with the title of my books on a piece of paper and gave it to them.

My time interviewing these nice people left me with one huge question. Why do I still hike with the goons I hike with?

23 Simple, Quick Overnighter

I have seen videos of people doing overnighters, suspended in tents, hanging off the side of El Capitan. NO! No way! Are they cray-cray? I get fearful of falling off my two-inch air mattress. Overnighters are sketchy enough without adding stress to the ordeal. When you consider the additional burden of sleeping bags, tents, air mattresses, extra hydration, stove, fuel, food, more food, lots of food, and snacks, weight becomes a real problem. Not to mention sleeping in the natural environment of wild animals, ticks and mosquitoes. On top of all that is the potty problem. Who wants to go full Tarzan in the middle of the night when your tummy is acting up, and what you thought would be a quick, stop and drop, turns into the Hershey highway. It ain't pretty, folks. Dave once went for a potty break and we didn't see him for two whole days. When we finally found him, he was dehydrated, malnourished, bug-bitten and poop-covered. We had to wash him off with a hose. Very sad.

Speaking of Dave, he and I wanted to break into the early spring weather with some simple, quick overnighters to start the year off. Problem was that the weather did not want to cooperate. Rain every weekend for most of April. And May was just as bad. We decided to attempt the Greenway Trail on Memorial Day weekend, stretching around 50 miles from the summit of Mount Monadnock to the summit of Mount Sunapee. It was to be a four-day trip. Ian and his brother, Jobe, were going to go along. This would be especially helpful as Ian had already completed it on a solo hike in just three days the year before.

The plan was for Ian, Jobe and I to start early Friday, hike Monadnock, then do the four miles to the first shelter where we would wait for Dave who was coming from a half-day's work. He would leave his car at the state park, hike over Monadnock and meet us at the shelter around 5 p.m. There was a call for rain that would last seven hours on Saturday, when we were to complete an 18-mile day. I had already suggested we scrub our plans, and on the sunny days of Sunday and Monday, do an overnighter on some mountain peak. But alas, no. This group is not interested in sound reasoning as you will soon see.

Friday morning brought rain, drizzle and fog — not a good start. Ian's wife, Caroline, drove us to the Dublin trailhead. We stashed our large packs in the woods, taking a small pack with all our hydration. Jobe volunteered to carry it, which he did for about one third of the trip. I carried it the rest of the way. You ask, "Why didn't Ian carry it?" That would be a great question: why would a 30-year-old man let a 64-year-old grandfather carry a heavy pack? I have no answer. I do whatever I need to do to keep the team together. Near the summit, the drizzle, combined with the wind, was causing me to wipe my glasses every 60 seconds. I finally took them off just to see. Does that make sense? Heading down the rock was wet and slick. I had put my glasses back on, as being out of the wind kept them somewhat dry. I was out in front when I slipped and took a nasty fall. My right forearm sustained four grueling gashes that were bleeding. I wiped the blood away and never let the others know about it for fear they would insist on my seeing a doctor. I was just happy I had not broken my arm. A 50-mile hike with a broken arm would have been difficult even for me. Please know that I would never have hiked Monadnock in the rain had it not been for the fact we were ALL doing a summit-to-summit hike.

Back at the parking lot the weather cleared some and it became very humid. After slinging on our unbelievably heavy packs, we made it the four miles to the shelter without incident. Ian started whining about Dave getting Subway. He wanted me to call Dave to get a sub for him and his brother. While calling Dave, I unearthed what was the most despicable, unannounced change of plans I have ever experienced. Dave left work, only to return home and retrieve his bicycle which he transported to the town of Washington. He locked it up in front of the general store, drove 30 miles to Brown Road, then hiked one mile in to reach the shelter. His unbeknownst plan was to camp the first night, hike 18 miles, camp the second night, then bail and ride his bicycle back to his car and go home. The rest of us were stunned. Who would make those kinds of plans and not tell anyone? I would never have done Monadnock in the rain if I thought the four of us were not going to do the whole hike. Ian was so upset that even though 12 other people had arrived at the shelter area, he was throwing and kicking things, cussing up a storm. It took Jobe and I quite a while to calm him down before Dave arrived. It was like the set of Jerry Springer.

Ian and Jobe set up their hammocks while I set up in the shelter. Dave arrived, followed by a mom-and-daughter team who all set up in the shelter. That night Dave and the mom started a "who could snore the loudest contest," which Dave clearly won. I got a solid 2.5 to three hours sleep. The rest of the night I listened to the rain and Rip Van Winkle. When I awoke, Dave was heating some coffee and had half his stuff already packed. By the time I heated my breakfast, Dave had his pack filled and was standing with his arms folded as if saying "Let's get moving." The thought of hiking 18 miles in the rain, then setting up camp in the rain, while being rushed by the guy who was going to bail was more than I could take with only three hours of sleep. I calmly announced I was calling Darlene to come and get me and they could enjoy the hike without me. I knew that was a low blow as there is no enjoyment in a hike without me. Ian started his kicking, throwing and cussing, while Dave started crying. It was all pathetic. Jobe was the only calm, cool-headed guy in the group.

Ian had called Caroline to come and get us. The mood was somber. I took full responsibility for ruining everyone's plans. We are a tight group; we overcome differences and keep our friendships strong. Even though that was the worst thought-out plan, without any kind of truthful communication, I absorbed everyone's pithy attitudes. That is what friends do,

I plan on attempting the Greenway Trail again in the fall. Probably do it solo.

24 THE SANDWICH DOME MAKEUP TEST

I remember getting an F on a math final. The teacher insisted I retake the test a week later, which I did, and got another F. He was so beside himself he gave me a D just so I could pass and asked that I never again attend his class. I don't know why he didn't like me; I was the only one offering comic relief from the boredom of math. I have previously confessed that while completing the 52 With a View list, that I never actually summited Sandwich Mountain, which is the highest of the 52. I missed it by 200 feet. We attempted a winter makeup test and failed again. This was our third attempt. While this is not a story about an overnighter, or a winter hike, or a solo hike, it is a story of making good on your word. All you really have in life is the reputation of your good word and, unlike Ian, Dave or Keith, my word is my bond.

I had recently bought my daughter's old car that had 220,000 miles for $500 and christened it the new hiking car. It is good on gas, but it has many issues that give it character. The doors don't always lock, the radio goes on and off at will, and the console navigation and camera system doesn't work, but it runs well and gets us to where we want to go. This was the first time in five months that Keith, Dave, Ian and I would be together on a hike. I was pretty excited yet concerned about my abilities as I have put on a few pounds and was a little unconditioned. I kept it to myself, and we all got into the classy auto and had a great ride north.

At the trailhead we found only five other cars. I guessed the high gas prices were starting to have an impact on the hiking community. We geared up and headed in.

The night before, it had rained and I knew the trail would be wet. After falling from wet rock on Monadnock I had lost my confidence in hopping rocks. The humidity was awful and made breathing difficult. It also added to the slipperiness of the rocks, so I avoided them as much as possible. Unfortunately, after a moderate start we encountered the steep, rocky sections heading to Noon Peak. I slowed my pace and chose my footing carefully. No sense to rush it. Besides, my heart rate was elevated to heart attack levels, my breathing was like a lady panting in childbirth and sweat was pouring out of me like a washcloth being wrung. Just then a guy goes flying by us, pushing like a bodybuilder on a steroid high. This guy was dang near running up the steeps. WTH! I am all for professional athletes, just not while I am hiking. It makes me question why I cannot do that. Oh, that's right, I have no desire to ever push myself that hard unless there is a 400-pound black bear on my butt. Even then it would be questionable.

I had forgotten my phone at home and that put me in a bit of a bad mood because I really wanted to get epic pics of the hike as it was the third attempt. I knew the stuff the goons would take would be third-grade level at best. I was overjoyed when at the best overview on the ridge a couple showed up who graciously took a group photo of the four of us. I knew they would turn out nice and they did. The overall ridge walk was somewhat level and pleasant. I was recuperating from the steep pull up. When we arrived at the junction that shoots off 0.2 mile to Jennings Peak, Ian decided to hold back as he had already completed it. Not wanting him to be lonely and having already done it myself, I decided to let Dave and Keith go it alone. Not wanting to just stand around for them to do the out and back, Ian and I decided to head to Sandwich Dome knowing we would take flak from the others — and we did. I am not sure why they were so testy. I was going quite slow and they summitted only a few minutes after us. Still, they complained and carried on like spoiled, bratty kids who had to clean their rooms.

For some unknown scientific reason, the flies at the top were a real menace. House flies by the hundreds. I did not know if it was normal or if Keith had not taken a bath. A passing storm threatened, then broke east. We had some refreshments and headed out. On the way down we ran into a fair share of hikers. We broke off to do the loop and descended by way of the Drakes Brook Trail.

I was extremely happy to have finally completed the summit and cleared my conscience.

The trail down was not as steep, but steep enough for the long distance. After joining up to the brook the going was level for 1.5 miles all the way out. Nearing the end of the 8.2-mile trip, my knees were getting stiff. I am so happy Sandwich Dome is not a 4,000-footer as it is only 3,992 feet high. Those last 8 feet would have been too much. Getting to the parking lot, we found it jammed-packed with cars parked along the driveway and another 15 cars parked along the highway. I guess the price of gas is not as big a deterrent as I had thought.

The goons were begging for a Dunkin' stop, which of course made me drive by it as if I had not heard their shouts. I am a jerk; I will be the first to admit it. All in good fun, I turned around and the babies got the bottle. The things I put up with.

After I was home, the pics started coming in and, sure enough, the only good ones were the four taken by the courteous couple. Still, I was relieved to know I had completed my makeup test, even if I only got a D-minus.

25 OSCEOLA
Overnighter

At 4,328 feet, Osceola is a moderate, semi-easy hike. Still, for an overnighter, there is a lot of added weight for all the gear necessary. For this reason, I put up significant resistance to Dave's and Ian's pleading to go. The goons finally wore me down by begging, crying and reminding me that hiking without me is just not as fun. I needed more overnighters for this book and that was the only reason I decided to go.

After loading my pack, I immediately started regretting it. I knew the weight would hurt my shoulders, back, hips, knees, feet, toenails and feelings — the latter being the worst. Half of that weight was the mega bologna sandwich and snacks I packed. I had researched weather reports and was shocked when I read that windchills would bring the nighttime temps to the high 30's. I knew I would need extra carbs for heat. I packed a dry T-shirt, gloves, hat and a puffy jacket, as well as my 0° F sleeping bag, a foam ground pad, an air mattress and air pillow. You need to know that a zero-degree bag means that you will be comfortable at 30°. I am all about comfort, especially when I do not want to fall asleep to the sound of chattering teeth.

The goons started kidding me about not reimbursing me for fuel. What used to cost $36 to fill my tank was now $83. I knew they were only joking, so I kind of felt bad driving off and leaving them at Subway. All in fun.

The drive north included the usual banter about solving the world's problems. We arrived at an almost full parking lot. I was fearing that there would be crowds of campers at the summit. We started in with me on point. The trail has a lot of rocks. It is not a smooth gravel path as some would be fooled into thinking. As we headed up, we met lots of people coming down. I soon realized we would be the only nuts sleeping out in near-winter conditions at the end of June. After my fall on Monadnock, my biggest fear was hiking on wet rock. To my horror, it was all wet with water running down the trail most of the way. Being cautious and taking our time kept us from harm. The pace I had set was perhaps a little too fast and all three of us were soaked with sweat. This didn't bode well as we summited and were hit by the 20 mph winds. We quickly changed into some dry clothing and set about selecting our camping site. Ian and I were inclined to camp in the woods because we expected people would be coming up for the sunrise. Dave was pouting about not camping on the ledges. At one point I saw him wipe some tears. He reluctantly decided to join us after I pointed out most bear attacks happen on ledges. It turned out to be a good decision as a young couple arrived at the summit at 2 a.m.

We turned in early as it was much too chilly to just hang out on the ledges. It took a few minutes for temps to rise in our sleeping bags. The wind was crashing into the side of the mountain causing the trees to sway and slam into each other like drunken punk rockers in a mosh pit. I noticed a dead pine directly in front of us. If it came down, it would hit Dave and myself. I pointed it out to Dave . . . Dave?

He was out like a baby with a belly of warm milk. Soon all three of us were in dreamland. I awoke to tinkle and, after getting back into my warm bed, decided to do what I always do... give the goons a late-night call. They were on to me; both their phones were set on silent. I left messages anyway. It's what I do.

I was awakened by the sounds of voices and lights flashing back and forth. Another party of six had arrived to greet the sunrise. We packed fast and joined both parties on the ledges. Ian and I got our stoves out and started heating our Mountain House breakfast meals and coffee. Dave went off on his own as all he brought was measly oatmeal and did not want to smell the aroma of the delicious meals Ian and I were enjoying.

The sun made a grand entrance and photo sessions were in full swing. I discovered the group of five women and one young man were from Bosnia. One girl insisted on having her picture taken with me after discovering I was the author of books that I had been trying to sell her for the last five minutes. I have no shame.

We said our goodbyes to the happy hikers and headed out. We were overjoyed to have experienced an awesome overnighter and spectacular sunrise. I was thrilled to not have frozen to death.

We met a lot of people who were heading up. Being on point, I always make sure we abide by hiking protocol allowing hikers ascending the right of way. Dave usually goes through them like a 10-pin bowling ball set on a strike.

Working our way out, the talk turned to my blanket. That's right, I have a favorite blanket. Don't judge me. Linus in the Charlie Brown cartoons carries a security blanket, and he is kind and polite. The goons were going at me pretty heavy, but I paid them no mind because they are both dog owners. I simply reminded them that, like a dog, my blanket is a companion . . . yet it does not bark, needs no food or water, does not pee or poop, never pukes, needs no shots, does not shed and never needs a vet visit. Don't judge me. You know, I might point out that maintaining mental health is a real thing and whatever a person needs to get through life should be accepted. After all, I accept the goons and still do overnighters with them even when they bring up my blanket. On the other hand, Darlene draws the line when I act like my blanket and I converse. In the words of Billy Joel, "You may be right, I may be crazy."

26 Ducks, Deer, Bear & Solo Hiking

For Father's Day, my daughter gave me a cool decal that I immediately placed on the back of the hiking car. It says *Always hike with someone in worse shape than you.* The problem is that I am that someone. Everyone wants to hike with me because it makes them feel better about themselves. While I am huffing and puffing, they are chatting and carrying on pleasant conversation. That is why I occasionally escape the in-shape-crowd to solo hike. I move at my pace. If you can imagine an old man using a walker, then put that scene on slow motion, you get the idea of "my pace".

The forecast for southern New Hampshire was 90° with humidity. Up north, it would be marginally cooler. I was mentally gearing up to do Mount Hight in the Carter Range, but Ian pleaded with me to wait until we could all go together so I decided to hike the faithful Belknap loop. I knew I would have to leave early to hike in the cool of the day.

I usually do not procrastinate. Why put off till tomorrow what you can put off for good? However, on the night before, I got enamored watching YouTube videos of bear attacks. Bears attacking moose, bison, elk, wolves, deer — even close encounters with humans. I do not know why I feed my overactive imagination with stuff like that before a solo hike. After living my whole life in New Hampshire, the only times I have seen a bear was while hiking Mount Moosilauke with Keith, and when I did my first solo hike on Mount Whiteface. Though the latter sighting was in my car as the bear ran out in front of me, I was only a half mile from the trailhead and could see in its eyes he knew where I was going and was racing there ahead of me.

I had awakened a little later than planned, made my coffee, grabbed my gear and headed out. I spotted something down the road that I could not identify. As I got closer, it turned out to be a female duck with six little ducklings all waddling down the center of the road like they owned the place. Their performance gave me a chuckle. I love the antics of wildlife. About halfway into the journey there are some fields so, as usual, I scanned them for deer. Nothing. A mile farther there was a large doe standing right in the middle of the road. She hopped into the woods as I got closer. After seeing these animals, I thought "this is going to be a great hike." A short distance from the trailhead I came over a hill and there he was. A large black bear was lumbering across the road heading for Gunstock Mountain. I suspected he was heading for elevation to enjoy cooler temps while hunting for breakfast. While he was a spectacular sight and part of me was saying "that's freaking awesome'" the other part of me was saying "Why? Why on a solo hike, after watching 20 minutes of bears-eating-things video?" Bears look roly-poly, but in reality are all muscle and attitude. They are incredibly fast and nimble and if it gets down to fisticuffs you are going to lose.

I calmed my imagination and comforted myself with the knowledge that I had just purchased a small dispenser of pepper spray. I have seen people with bear spray bottles that look like fire extinguishers. They look like they weighed five pounds and can probably spray 40 feet for a full 10 minutes. What are people thinking? I purchased a Sabre Red pepper spray that I am guessing holds two ounces of spray and will last all of five seconds. It is one of those key-ring types that women buy to fend off people like Keith, Dave and Ian. I know what you are thinking. You are thinking, "Ken, will that be enough to deter an angry bear starving for breakfast?" Here is where everyone makes a common mistake. The spray is not for the bear. What you are supposed to do is spray yourself directly in both eyes, then your eyes will burn themselves shut and you will not be able to see what the bear will do to you. Also, you will be in so much agony you will actually wish the bear rips your head off to end the pain. See how easy life is. This response is for solo hiking. If you are with someone else, the objective is to spray them, then watch as they run screaming right into the claws of the waiting bear who will appreciate you for seasoning its lunch. Hiking is not complicated, folks.

By the way, the hike was epic. Not only did I not have to deal with a bear, but I did not have to deal with the goons. It was a win-win situation.

27 KEARSARGE NORTH
4th of July Solo Hike

Though I had been invited to a large family Fourth of July cookout with evening fireworks, I had other plans for my holiday. A nice peaceful solo hike. Keith was camping in his Motel 6 on wheels, Dave went to an evening concert and wanted to rest, and Ian was at a cabin up in Maine. That left me with a chance to be alone in the north woods of New Hampshire.

There is a different level of seriousness when I prepare for a solo hike. The day before, I checked all the weather reports. They revealed temps in the 80's with high humidity and a mild breeze. Hiking in heat and humidity had gotten me in trouble before, so I knew I needed to do two things: leave early to beat the heat and make sure I had enough hydration. Leaving early meant getting up at 3:45 a.m. to start my hike at 6 a.m. and hydration meant no less than three liters with another 16 ounces in the car waiting for me. I also go over everything in my pack with a different level of scrutiny. Proper clothing, medical and repair items, and plenty of snacks. When I started this hike, it was 60° F and humid. When I was coming down it was in the 80's and very humid. Out of all the hydration I started with I was left with only about 12 ounces. On the way out I saw an older couple heading up with no gear and each carrying a 16 oz. bottle of water. That is a recipe for disaster. Believe me, I know!

I am usually more pumped and in the zone when I solo. As I placed my gear, coffee, and bug spray in the car, my heightened senses noticed the crisp morning air, the sound of peepers, and the brilliance of the star-soaked sky. Within the first two miles of travel, I noticed something in the road ahead of me. It appeared to be an animal, but I could not make it out. As I got closer, the headlights revealed not one animal but two. Two foxes that broke off what they were doing and ran off in opposite directions. Years ago, the Beatles wrote a song entitled *Why Don't We Do It in the Road*. These foxes took that as a challenge!

This was to be the first time in a while that I traveled up Route 16. I quickly remembered why I avoid it. It is mostly only two lanes, and if you get stuck behind someone who thinks doing the speed limit is a virtue you are in for a long drive. I was fortunate in that I was so early there was little traffic.

The first time I hiked North Kearsarge was a winter hike with Keith and Ian. I remembered the summit was picturesque but did not remember much else. My mind had blocked out the pain. This mountain is 3,269 feet high with 2,600 feet of elevation gain. The stroll up is 3.1 miles, but the first .6 mile is flat, meaning that you gain 2,600 feet of elevation in about 2.5 miles. That is one long, incredibly steep 2.5 miles!

Because I detest the tranquility of a hike being shattered by the incessant barrage of the little winged demon bugs of New Hampshire, I covered myself in enough bug spray to stop a full-on bear attack and headed into the woods. Oh, to enjoy the sights and sounds of the forest. The trail started off by going through a hardwood forest, the decaying leaves of the previous year omitting a smell that reminded me of a hay loft. Either that or I was hallucinating from the fumes of the bug spray. The morning was chilly and my senses were alive to my surroundings. A loud sound to my left got my attention. Most people would immediately think a squirrel or raccoon, but no, with me ... a bear or charging moose, or my sixth-grade history teacher Sister Hellens, who was going to grill me on the historical facts of the Fourth of July! False alarm, just a squirrel. The birds were filling the forest with their morning songs, one sounding just like the bird in the *Hunger Games*, "May the odds be ever in your favor."

The trail was steep and "boney," (a term used to describe lots of rock) About halfway up it turned to solid bedrock, which allowed for an easier stride. As you got closer to the summit, it got really steep and turned back to lots of roots and rocks. It was at this time that my foot got wedged between a root and rock and I could not get it out. I was pulling and trying to lift it out to no avail. This was when I was really thankful that I was solo hiking because the goons would have taken pictures and had lots of laughs at my expense. Right before I got desperate enough to untie my boot and get my foot out, I gave it a strong push forward and it dislodged. That is the first time that has ever happened. It was around this time that I had noticed I was close to the summit because everywhere I looked I could see daylight through the trees, yet I kept hiking up. For the next half-mile it appeared as if I would break summit, yet the trail only got steeper and kept on going. I was sure I was witnessing some seismic activity that was pushing the summit cone upwards as I was hiking. I don't know, maybe it was the bug spray.

Finally arriving at the summit, I saw a young couple who had camped on the rocks and two guys who had camped inside the fire tower. I walked the summit area and took pics. It did not seem to have the same allure it did on the winter hike. I hung out for a few minutes, drank a protein shake and headed down.

I met another couple hiking up and we chatted a while and they agreed about the illusion of the summit. They readily agreed it seemed to keep growing taller the higher up you hiked. After I left them, the couple who had camped out came down behind me and, as they passed me, I noticed the guy had a large daypack with stuff hanging off it, but the woman had a pack that reached above her head and below her butt. Of course, having no filter, I just blurted out "Hey, how come she's carrying the heavy pack?" Well, that started a fun conversation about how they were brand-new to hiking and she was able to find an overnight pack on Facebook Marketplace but he, as of yet, had not. Then out of nowhere they asked, "Aren't you the author that has written two humorous books on hiking with all the profits going to New Hampshire Search and Rescue?" Haha, I am amazed how many hikers have ESP. We conversed for a while and then they shot off down the trail like deer, with their long-limbed fit bodies. Jerks! Haha, Darlene used to say I was a diamond in the rough. After 38 years, she has the diamond and is left with just the rough.

I met another couple coming up and the gentleman was not wearing a shirt. Far be it for me to ever judge, but I will no longer hold a bad self-body image. Then again, it could be the bug spray.

28 Mount Moosilauke
Solo

Darlene was supposed to babysit the grandkids, leaving me with nothing to do on a Friday. The forecast for higher elevations that day was in the mid-50's with a 10-mph breeze. Perfect conditions! I had just hiked three days before and my legs had not fully recovered, but I figured what the heck, I'm rugged. I figured wrong.

Once again, all my hiking companions were unavailable, which did not bother me as I needed a few more solo hikes for the book. Not only that, but I am actually starting to enjoy solo hiking.

I was up at 3:45 a.m. and started the two-hour drive to the trailhead. Other than seeing a fox, the drive was boring. I played the Ian card by Googling the easiest ascent, it pointed me to the Gorge Brook Trail. The road in knocks off some elevation, leaving only 2,400 feet in a 3.7-mile hike. This was going to be great. Easy and great.

At the parking lot, I met a young couple who were drinking their morning coffee. We chatted a bit, then I headed up. Dang, this was one of the boniest, boulder-strewn trails I have ever been on. Now I know why the trail description said this hike requires five hours. There was no way to make good time without blowing out an ankle. There was morning fog and humidity, making breathing difficult. The trail may have been moderate, but I was panting like a dog locked in a heated car. Sweat was pouring off my forehead, while my torso and arms were cold from the morning chill. My legs started reminding me that the extra weight I put on was pissing them off and they were not going to take it. This was turning into a killer. I had crossed three bridges on the way up and, at times, the trail flattened out and no longer had the rocks from hell to tiptoe through. There were a few spots with running water on the trail then back to boulders everywhere, but at least the fragrance of the evergreens was soothing. I hit a lengthy section of flat trail and hit a nice stride. It did not last long as it got steep and ridiculously rocky. This hike was turning out to be as fun as a proctologist appointment.

I decided I needed some energy, so I stopped, hydrated and ate a Stinger protein bar. Just then the young couple I had met at the trailhead showed up. The woman said "There you are, we were wondering when we would catch up to you. You were making some really good time." I cannot tell you how good that made me feel. I realized it was not just rocks and humidity. I guess I was pushing harder than I realized. I never get compliments from the goons I hike with. It is always harping and picking, "You're going too fast, you're going too slow, you're farting again ..." OK, I can own the last one. Propel Water does something to my gut and if it annoys the goons, then why not? It is a way of getting even for all the nonstop abuse I put up with. Nonetheless, the compliment was encouraging. I think everyone can use a good encouraging comment from time to time. You should think of someone right now, then call them and encourage them to buy this book.

I returned the encouragement to this kind lady and, after promising they would buy my book, I let the couple go past me. I looked at my trail guide and saw I had one mile left to go and it was going to get steep. Trail workers had built a rock staircase right up a half-mile steep section. It made things a whole lot better, but still it was a workout. The trail flattened out again, then broke treeline, revealing the last half mile with moderate elevation to the summit.

At the summit, I filmed a gear review for the *White Mountain Approved* YouTube channel. I filmed it about my two-liter, Camelback hydration bladder. I have had it for years and it keeps going strong. If you are looking for a bladder, I highly recommend Camelback. When you fill it with Propel it is fartastic. (I can hear my eldest sister now, "Kenneth, stop it." Hahaha.)

Heading down, the heat had risen a few degrees and the humidity was oppressive. My legs were tired, so I busted out my hiking poles for a little more stability. It was now about 9:30 a.m. and the hiking parade was in full swing. No less than 45 hikers of every age and nationality were making their way up Moosilauke. Some were smiling and chatting, while some were visibly struggling. Some had kids, some had dogs, some were going solo. I was amazed that the high cost of gas had not dampened their love for hiking. I guess it is worth the extra expense when you are making memories.

Back at the car I had clocked in exactly five hours. After the two-hour ride home, my legs had solidified like cement and I had a hard time walking ... ah yes, memories!

On the way home, I hit a cat. I was devastated. I went to the house, informed the woman at the door what happened and offered to replace the cat. She said, "OK, but how are you at catching mice?"

29 Trail Wisdom
Play It Safe When Solo Hiking

An acronym in the hiking community that helps hikers keep a cool head if they discover they are lost is called S.T.O.P. Below I will give you the true definition of terms followed by my interpretations.

If you get lost, STOP

S – Stay calm. Relax, sit down, take a sip of water, breathe slowly.

> (**S – Strip** yourself of all unnecessary weight that will slow your soon panicky running speed.)

T – Think. Get out your map and see what you can learn.

> (**T – Try** screaming as loud and long as you can, it makes you feel better to hear yourself lose control.)

O – Observe. Look for landmarks, look for footprints.

> (**O – Obey** every crazy thought that comes into your mind, like tearing off all your clothes and drinking that puddle of slime underneath the rotting blowdown.)

P – Plan. If you know the route, go carefully and mark your trail along the way. If you're really unsure, stay in one place. It's a rule of the woods. You're easier to find that way. Periodically blow your whistle three times. Three blasts of the whistle are an international distress call.

> (**P – Pee** yourself, it's going to happen anyway. Human urine is a natural deterrent to wild animals; besides, you already ditched the whistle when you stripped yourself of your gear.)

Some other tidbits . . .

Common sense says, "Let someone know your planned hike, as well as trails taken and time of return."

(Great advice until you are running late and drive by that God forsaken mountain you have always wanted to try. Why drive another hour when there is a perfectly good mountain that will save driving time and get you in the woods sooner? Besides, search-and-rescue folks love the challenge of looking for someone. It's kind of like adult hide-and-seek.)

The nut jobs I hike with always intend to be out of the woods before nightfall.

(This is so true. Remember the higher you go, the faster the sun will set because of the gained altitude, but always remember, even if it sets on you, it will be back in a few hours. Have some patience for crying out loud!)

When obeying the Ten Essentials rule you should always have extra food and water in case something goes wrong.

(What can go wrong? A piece of gum keeps the jaws going and tricks the mind into thinking you are constantly eating, also it helps hydration by swallowing your own spit that your saliva glands are pumping out in gallons. Gum, rather than food, saves weight also.)

When I solo hiked Mt. Liberty in the winter, Darlene was concerned no one else would be on the trail.

(You are solo hiking because you don't want to see other people. Also, if you are in bear country, other hikers just attract more attention. Stay remote, stay isolated, stay safe.)

Always follow the blazes. I have done my fair share of clearly marking trails with easy-to-follow blazes to help hikers stay on course.

(Remember, blazes that look like skull and crossbones mean no pirates on that trail. Also, some "Turn Back" warnings are just because trail maintenance crews are lazy and don't want people messing up their trail. Never wander off, unless you see a hotdog stand. Sure it may be a dehydration induced mirage, but hey, it's hotdogs!)

Some hikers wear bear bells.

(If you stay quiet you have a better chance of sneaking up on a sleeping bear. Think of the great pics you will get.)

Don't wear earbuds.

(You will not be able to hear a bear charging and won't have time to relieve yourself. Again, the smell of human excrement is a natural deterrent.)

You will learn a lot about yourself.

(Like the fact that you are a chicken, coward, scaredy-cat who should have thought twice about going into the woods alone.)

Here is a real-life occurrence that happened to my hiking buddies, Moe, Larry, and Curly, when they got lost. It happened as they managed to get off trail while hiking Mt Owls Head in the center of the Pemigewasset wilderness. The first brainstorm they got was to split up so they could find their way out faster. As fortune would have it, Ian was the first one to find a trail and work his way out. Two days later his 911 call was sent out from a local Dunkin Donuts. I know, I know. Let's just leave that one alone. Next was the ever-rational Keith, who immediately set out to remain in place and wait for rescue. He built a crude shelter out of twigs and leaves, then started a signal fire that burnt down 100 acres. Needless to say he was soon rescued as the International Space Station saw the inferno and called NH SAR. Lastly was Dave who is unable to stay in place anywhere longer than five minutes. Well, good old Dave decided if he walked in a straight line he would eventually find civilization. Two months later he was discovered by Royal Canadian Mounted Police riding a moose while clothed in a black bear skin and wearing a raccoon hat. What a crew.

30 Liar, Liar, Pants on Fire

I woke at 5 a.m. with concerned thoughts about the day's hike. A recent weight gain and lack of conditioning had made my past few hikes unpleasant I had been eating better and working out, so was hoping this trip would be easier. Blueberry Mountain is not a tough mountain.

Snowshoes! Dang, I hate snowshoes. We had received another six inches of snow, so I had to bring them. My hope was that the trail would be broken out.

I drove to Keith's house, moved my gear into his truck and we set off for Concord where we met Ian, loaded into his car and headed north. The conversation was enjoyable. Since it was a Friday, Dave could not go with us, and he was none too happy about it. Arriving at the trailhead, we found "No Parking" signs everywhere. Though there was a small parking area 100 feet up the road, Ian decided he would drive a quarter mile up a steep hill and park in a large parking lot for Mt. Moosilauke.

After hiking down the hill we had to hike back up the dirt road to the trailhead only to discover an unbroken trail. With the joy of snowshoes on my feet, I stepped onto the trail to find there was a one-inch crust that you easily punched through and sunk five inches into powder. Dear God in heaven. I broke trail for the first quarter mile and was dead in my tracks. One snowshoe had come off so I ditched the other one and found there was no difference in bare-booting. Ian took the lead and I followed for another quarter mile. The engine that ran my legs sputtered and skipped, hiccupped and coughed, and then with a wheeze, gave up the ghost and died. I was Bonked! I got Ian's keys and started the walk of shame back to the car knowing I would never hear the end of this debacle. In perspective, that was no easy hike in those conditions.

After going stir crazy in the car I took a half mile hike up the trail leading to Mt Moosilauke. It was packed down and a lot easier going. Returning to the car it was only a short while before Keith and Ian arrived.

As we headed home, I was told, "It's a good thing you turned around, you would have never made the summit. The snow conditions were brutal." I knew I would never live this one down. Until…

Two days later, still licking my wounds, I was scrolling through the 52 With A View Facebook page and lo and behold what did my eyes land upon??? A post from a woman who said, "Hiked Blueberry Mountain today. Found the trial broken out to the overview. We broke out the rest of the trail to the summit." I had to re-read the post three times in disbelief. I was speechless. "Good thing you didn't summit Ken." "It was brutal Ken." "You'd have never made it Ken!!!"

Liar, Liar, Marmot Scree winter hiking pants on fire!

Why can't people be more truthful like me?

31 THE HOLT TRAIL

When You Have an Injury, But Not Too Many Brains

After five excruciating solo hikes in just under four weeks, my right knee seized up like The Tin Man without oil. Bending it back was impossible. The knee made clickety-clackety sounds like an engine getting ready to blow. I used ice, Aleve, Advil and stayed off it for two weeks.

After all the TLC, I was at approximately 80 percent. It still felt a little swollen. I had been wanting to solo Mount Hight in the Carter Range, but I felt nine miles would push the knee too far. So what did I do? I called Keith and said I was going to hike the Holt Trail up Mount Cardigan, one of the most difficult trails in New England.

I was shocked when Keith said he would go. I had watched a YouTube video of two hikers going up the Holt Trail and was not fully convinced I wanted to attempt it. I decided it would be better to not share too much information with Keith. He is 73 and I did not want to give him a heart attack, I figured it would be better to save that for the trail.

I had hiked every trail up Cardigan except the Holt Trail, so it had been on my bucket list for some time. Dave had hiked it and warned me it was steeper than anything I had ever done. Seeing as Dave never warns anyone about any trail ever, he had my attention. Still, I saw no problem hiking a difficult trail with a bum knee, because, well … I am a bonehead. We all do dumb things from time to time, but injuries should be a red flag when planning hikes. I mean, I usually have to take into consideration, when hiking with the goons, the extent of their brain injuries.

The night before I only got three-and-a-half hours of sleep. Add that to a bum knee and the extra 30 pounds I had put on, what could go wrong?

I awoke at 4 a.m., made a light breakfast and coffee. Keith arrived at my house at 5 a.m. and we headed out. Our senior moment came when we realized our memory of directions was leading us to the west side. It was time for Google Maps. After some backroad adjustments we found ourselves at the AMC Cardigan Lodge.

The morning air was cool and refreshing. We put on our packs and headed up. The first 1.6 miles was mostly flat. We arrived at the junction and read the warning sign. We were not deterred. The next 0.5 mile were moderate and then the trail became steep as it followed a mostly dried stream bed. Out of nowhere, we were confronted with a steep slab rock with a deep crack running up it. The mossy rock was slippery, and I struggled for quite a while with no success. Keith was content to sit on a rock and watch the entertainment. Fortunately, there was a short bushwhack around it and we were back in the game.

The trail became one ridiculously steep section after another. Keith and I were both breathing hard from exertion and adrenaline. The ordeal was only beginning. The sections became more frequent and steeper. I concluded that we had covered too much to turn around — it was all or nothing. We hit some areas that had us on all fours, then others that had us clinging to boulders for dear life. I was now crying and Keith was mumbling to himself something about never listening to me again. Every now and then the trail mercifully presented areas where you could sit and rest ... and pray. Keith developed some kind of tic that made his head lunge forward as he hiccupped and snorted all at once, then his leg would twitch and he would say, "Ah, ah, ah, ah, ah." Poor old guy, all I could do was look away so as not to make him feel self-conscious.

Who in their right mind decided that going up vertical cliff for 0.7 of a mile would be fun? We lost the trail once. Keith bushwhacked while I went down to where we missed it. Right when he yelled that he found the trail I discovered this insanely steep slab that he had avoided. I scrambled up like a lunatic. Then, all at once, it appeared ...

The section wasn't steep, it was impossible. There was a protruding section of slab rock that seemed to offer the only sane way up, as it offered possible hand holds. There was no way you could go up this section without it. I thought I was hallucinating and double-checked to see if we were on the trail. Looking down the trail I saw brown trail blazes, then I realized they were not blazes, but places where people had crapped themselves, with me leaving the freshest boom-boom.

I started up, got halfway, and could not find any hand holds or foot holds. The rock was so steep I was holding my weight with my hands, gripping the protruding boulder. Going back down was not an option. When I glanced back at Keith 35 feet below me, his eyes were bulging out as he inherently knew if I fell, I would be taking him out like a linebacker. The longer I stayed, frantically looking for anything that would help, the more my arms grew tired. The only possibility was to put all my weight on a two-finger grip I had found while I lifted my left knee up onto the top of the boulder. The problem was my right foot had slipped twice already and if it slipped during the daring attempt, I would be going for a 35-foot fall down this section. I think I had an out-of-body experience, saw my life pass before my eyes and heard a voice calling my name. Turns out it was Keith saying, "Would you get going? I'm getting bored down here." I prayed a very sincere prayer, promised God all kinds of new devotion and lifted myself up and out. The adrenaline was so intense I did not even feel the cuts and bruises I was giving my left knee. I hit the rest of the slab rock and moved so fast up on all fours that I did not even give my feet an opportunity to slip.

I felt bad leaving Keith behind, but it was so steep that he could not help me, and I could not help him. When I got to the top, where I could actually stand upright, I turned to see Keith just making his way over that crazy boulder in the same fashion I had done. Reunited, I noticed both our left knees were cut and bleeding.

We did a few more short scrambles that in the past would have made us pucker, but now seemed like child's play. The next thing we knew we were looking at the tower on the summit. We walked upright up a section most people would crawl. Oh, how I was hoping there would be the usual crowd of people, who upon seeing us come over that crest would stop and stare in admiration. But, alas, no, not a soul.

Keith and I congratulated ourselves on overcoming our fears and pushing through an unforgettable hike. Then it occurred to me that my bum knee had been scared painless. All the stiffness and discomfort were gone. I had officially scared it straight.

If you ever suffer a knee injury, I highly recommend you DO NOT take the Holt Trail!!!

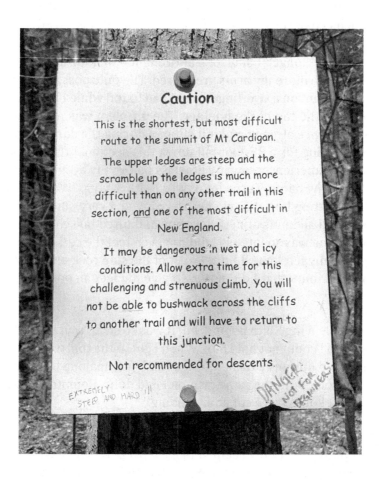

32 Boy, You're Gonna Carry That Weight

OK, OK, I know that some of these stories do not line up with the title of the book, but they have a value ... of sorts ... I guess ... I am the author here, so keep reading!

All my life I have been a big fan of The Beatles. One of their songs from the 1969 album, *Abbey Road*, is called *Carry That Weight*. As I said earlier, 2022 was a bad winter for me and I had officially put on 30 pounds. I was not proud of myself because I knew how good I felt when I had previously lost it. I also knew that it made hiking a lot more difficult having to "Carry That Weight." This was one of the reasons I wanted to solo hike because I knew my pace was not what it once had been.

For the second time I was set to hike Mount Hight. Dave was begging me to hike with him because I had done so much solo hiking that the goons were sad to have lost my expert guide qualifications, along with my lifesaving skills, and great sense of humor. Can't say I blame them. We decided to hike Hight.

Dave showed up at my house at 4:40 a.m. and we started the long drive north. Even at the early hour I could tell the humidity was going to be brutal. What I did not know was the temps would be 14° hotter than forecast, 100 percent humidity and without any breeze.

As we drove up Route 16, Dave started complaining about how long the drive to Hight was. Just then we were going past Mount Chocorua, and Dave casually said, "We can do that," as he pointed out the window. I had to admit it would save two hours of driving time. Oh, what the heck, why not? My last memory of Chocorua was a winter hike with Dave when I swore I would never hike with him again, never hike in winter again and never hike Chocorua again. Oh well, at least it was not winter.

Dave started bouncing up and down and giggling like a three-year-old that did his first potty in the can. All I was thinking about was carrying that extra 30 pounds up that God forsaken Piper Trail. The sky was blue, it was relatively cool, birds were chirping, and I was wondering why the heck I was even hiking. Just before it started getting steep, I thought I heard a moose grunting. Turns out I had forgotten that the day before I had eaten two servings of beans. Some little toots ripped out like a cannon blast while others were rapid fire like a machine gun. Dave was mumbling something under his breath as I assured him I had no control. The body has to do what the body has to do. I did happen to find some wild blueberries and ate them. I figured maybe some fruit would calm things down. They were small yet filled with flavor.

The whole drive up, and now on the hike, Dave was talking about his new Asolo boots he just bought. I had once had a pair and they are great boots. When we hit the steep, slab rock ledges he was amazed the boots had more stick than a kid with boogers on his fingers. He was flying up the rock like a mountain goat. I told him I was so happy he found something that actually made him faster. (Time to start solo hiking again)

The heat index was rising faster than Dave in his new boots, the humidity was killer, and the 30 extra pounds were making themselves known, I found myself needing to stop and rest quite a bit. Dave was fine with it until a little toot would appear and he was on the move again. We were making record time if you count "slowest" as a record. I was sucking hydration from my bladder tube like a diesel-powered Shop-Vac. I pushed through and eventually staggered to the summit.

We spent about 20 minutes on the summit until the next hiker arrived. As we headed down, Dave decided to try out his new Black Diamond hiking poles. He was duly impressed and said, "Now I know why you guys fly down these mountains." Once again, I was thrilled to know he found something to make him faster going down.

When we made our way to the slab ledges, we discovered they were now radiating heat like a blast furnace. Sweat was pouring out of us like oil from the Exxon Valdez, as The Beatles sang, "Boy, you're going to carry that weight a long time."

We got past the ledges when Dave snapped. It could have been the heat, dehydration, stress or that tiny little fart that sent birds flying from the trees. In all seriousness, Dave said, "You know PK, one of these days you are going to rip one and blow your intestines right out your rectum." Well, that made my day, and I laughed the next two miles. He is such a funny guy.

We met a lot of nice people as they were heading up and, back at the parking lot, we found it full of cars with license plates from all over the country.

On the drive home, Dave would not stop talking about digestive health and fiber supplements. He really is a funny guy. We stopped at a Dunkin' and found the lobby closed, so we got back in the car just as a lady was posting a "Store Closed" sign on the drive-thru intercom. She told us it was from a lack of staff. Where have all the workers gone? I need Dunkin' after a hike! Oh well, I guess we will all have to carry that weight ... until the next Dunkin'.

I hope Dave gets over his Borborygmus-phobia!

33 MOUNT PAUGUS
Solo Hiking Ghosts

The last four weeks had been hotter than two mice having whoopee in a wool sock in August. The humidity was so high, after stepping out of a shower you started sweating just reaching for the towel. People all over the state were hugging their air conditioners like they were relatives at an airport. Then, out of nowhere, a day in the 60's, with an easy breeze and little humidity, shrouded with a high elevation cloud cover, appeared like a rabbit from a magician's hat. I could not refuse.

Dave was busy rebuilding the front steps to his house, Keith was sleeping out in his camper trailer (I have a hard time calling that camping) and Ian was home with explosive diarrhea and hiccups. They left me with no alternative but to do a solo hike.

Two things that astound me about repression are how a woman can push a 10-pound baby out of a rather small opening while screaming threats of manslaughter to her husband and two hours later be all smiles and joy. And how I can hike a mountain and within a few months forget all about the near-death experience.

I vaguely remembered that the Kelley Trail heading up to Paugus had a spectacular section that goes through a narrow, enchanted canyon. Images of moss-covered blowdowns and square-cut boulder walls danced in my head. Paugus got my vote. AllTrails said it was a 7.7-mile round trip. AllTrails lies like Bill Clinton coming home at 1 a.m. Not only that, but their elevation rings do not come close to reality. I will bet they could make the Grand Canyon look like a small depression.

My alarm sounded at 4 a.m., I made coffee and had Cheerios for breakfast. OK, just one Cheerio. OK, fine, I had a doughnut! I gathered up my gear and headed out. The drive was pleasant. I was contemplating the mood of the hike without the goons, no one to pick on how I had dressed, no one to bust on my driving techniques, no one to complain about my pace, no one to lose it if I accidentally tooted.

I arrived at the parking lot at 6:30 a.m. and started up the Old Mast Trail and soon turned at the junction onto the Kelley Trail. Then it happened. While enjoying my solitude I got a creepy feeling someone was behind me. Noises of footsteps kept me peering over my shoulder. As I hit the anticipated canyon he appeared. It was the phantom ghost of Ian!

I have come to believe that somehow between his massive squirts, he teleported into my subconscious mind. It was so real — burps, insults, endless stories — it was all so horribly life-like. Freaking out, I quickened my pace, yet how can you outrun a ghost? He started making fun about how I had forgotten that the trail dropped elevation like a rollercoaster. After I connected with the Lawrence Trail, he was pointing out that the trail was, in reality, 8.5 miles. When I accidentally sustained a jab wound on my right wrist, he pointed out that I have the balance of a drunken ballerina with vertigo. This was a nightmare.

Upon reaching the summit, I met a group of eight that had spent the night on the ledges. While talking to them about my books, the foul spirit seemed to have left. I ate my lunch and, using my pack as a pillow, laid out for some resting time. The hike had been harder than I had remembered and just when I believed the hallucination had subsided, I heard his voice say, "I'm ready to go when you are." Holy crapola, I grabbed my gear and started heading down super-fast. The hellish voice said, "Now we are making good time." On one steep section, I stepped on a wet rock and had a mild fall, only to hear the mocking voice say, "Careful!"

I sped past the Kelley Trail junction, taking the Lawrence Trail back to the Old Mast Trail. There was some elevation gain, causing the dark beast to say, "We should have taken the Kelley Trail." Once hitting the Old Mast Trail for the remaining two miles down I turned on the jets, attempting to distance myself from Diarrhea Demon Boy. It was no use. I completed the 8.5 miles in under four hours.

Once in my car, the radio helped dispel the madness until, when in Concord, the voice yelled "Take this exit!" It was a lie, followed by evil laughter. I finally made it home where the loving presence of Darlene seemed to send the spirit back to its porcelain throne.

I HAD forgotten how long that trail was, but it was still an awesome, somewhat solo hike, on a perfect morning.

(See Ian, this is what happens when you tell me you see a moose and you LIE!)

So, yeah, I am calling this a solo hike.

PS: As I was traveling down the Old Mast Trail, I met a hiker going up. I casually asked, "Where you headed?" He responded, "Don't know, just going up." Do not be "that" guy!

34 THE DEER FLY
Overnighter

As this book is written primarily for those who hike in the Northeast, you are probably all familiar with the incessant nuisance of the deer fly. When those little pests get onto you, they have you swatting and slapping and swinging your arms like a crazy person. They circle you like a turd going down the hopper, then, as fast as lightning, bite the living daylights out of you, leaving a hole big enough to need stitches.

This is what Dave is like when he gets it in his mind to do an overnighter. Weather be damned! He is as bothersome as a dog that just heard the refrigerator door open. He is like a nose drip on a winter hike that just will not stop. He ... you get the picture.

Friday into Saturday was perfect weather, but Dave and Ian made plans to go to a concert Friday evening. Dave, not wanting to miss a hiking opportunity, reached out to me about doing a Thursday overnighter. Seeing as we both had to work, this would be a partial night hike with headlamps. Besides that, the weather forecast was calling for a 50 percent chance of rain till 6 p.m., dropping to 15 percent till midnight, then partially clearing. The winds were forecasted at 35 mph. These conditions would be enough for me to talk my way out with any rational hiker, but Dave is not rational! He was Mr. Positivity. "Oh, it will be great." "We will get subs and eat on the summit." "The rain will never come; the sunrise will be awesome." "We'll bring our stoves and have hot coffee in the morning." By the end of the conversation, he was sobbing as if this was his last chance to hike before succumbing to paralysis.

At first, I thought we could sleep at lower elevation in tents, stay dry, then summit in the morning. Then I thought, the heck with it, we will summit, sleep on the ledges and, if it rains, we will get soaking wet and hike out at 1 a.m. and I will never let him live it down. Next time he starts the deer fly maneuver I will be like "Hey Dave, remember that overnighter on the ledges?"

I packed light. My goal was to hike, sleep, wake up, descend and go home. Easy.

He was supposed to meet me at my house at 4:30 p.m., but he showed up at 5 p.m. and so it began. We stopped at Subway, got dinner and he gave me directions going up backroads rather than connecting to the highway. It was like watching a train wreck in slow motion or dreaming one of those horrible dreams from which you cannot wake up.

We finally got to the trailhead and headed up. The humidity was what you would expect to find in the jungles of Southeast Asia. Water was pouring out of me like a busted water main. We knocked out a couple of miles when I discovered a minor inconvenience of not being able to breathe. I have never experienced anything like it. I was sounding like an old horse with the death rattle. I stopped every couple of hundred feet only to discover I could not recover until after I yawned. WTH! I pushed on. We hit a few hundred feet of flat trail and I was still sucking air like I had a plastic bag stuck in my windpipe. I pushed on. We were now using our headlamps as we came to the steep slab rock. I pushed on. I got a glimpse of how far the summit was and almost fainted, yet ... I pushed on. We hit the summit cone that puts the "eep" in steep. I pushed on. All this time Dave was talking about how much fun we were going to have.

We circled the summit cone looking for cover from the Category One hurricane winds. Dave found this ledge that had me sleeping under an evergreen bush and him on an inclined slab rock a few feet away. At first, he put his sleeping bag on a ground pad and started sliding like a Canadian toboggan run. I found the prospect of awakening and finding him four ledges down, needing an airlift, somewhat amusing.

We ate our supper and bedded down around 9:30 p.m. I awoke at 10:30 and noticed the sky filled with stars. "I'll be darned," I thought.

As I watched in admiration, I noticed star after star disappearing until within 45 minutes they were erased from the heavens. I checked out my doppler radar app and came face to face with a monster storm cell coming out of the north headed right for us. I did some quick calculations and determined by 2 a.m. we would be underwater.

Dozing only a few minutes, I would awake and view the doppler. The thought crossed my mind to pack up quietly, hike out, drive home, and then the next day hear how a hiker was washed away in a flash flood never to be seen again. I forced that out of my mind because Dave was nice enough to give me the better of the two sleeping spots. By 1 a.m. the super cell seemed to be in a struggle with the howling winds coming from the west. We were now caught in a massive wind turbine. The wind blowing through the fire tower uprights was screaming like a jet engine, flowing down the ledge and buffeting our sleeping bags like sails in a typhoon. Neither of us was getting any sleep.

Finally, at 2:30 a.m., the cell dissipated and was no more. The winds quieted down and I believed I could actually get an hour-and-a-half sleep. Dave started snoring.

I awoke in a puddle of my own drool. My sleeping bag smelled like a homeless person had crawled in and died and my body ached from using a thin sleeping pad on sheer rock.

The sun was making its appearance and, as I heated my coffee, I had to admit the night was freaking awesome. A few other hikers appeared with the sunrise. Dave and I packed up and headed out after I had snapped some award-winning pics.

Dave had melted his sleeping bag with his hot coffee cup and neither of us got any sleep, but we had grins on our faces and a sense of accomplishment. I know I will look back on this adventure with fondness. Still, the next time Dave has a hiking brainstorm I will be asking, "Where is the dang fly swatter?"

35 OLD AGE & HIKING

(Content is not for those who are easily offended on behalf of others)

I have been thinking about starting up a Fortune 500 company and have come up with the granddaddy of all ideas. I am going to start a hiking supply company for old timers. I am talking about those that came off the ark with Noah but are still around today ... and still hiking. I suspect 40 years from now Dave will still be hiking at 92 so I will use him as my typical customer. That way you do not have to think about your dear Nana or Poppa and get all testy with me.

Dave will be incontinent by then. Heck, he is already there now. What is the solution? Ken's Camo Colored Biodegradable Hiking Depends. A simple tape-on application inside your favorite hiking undies and, voila, a little dribble, a little drabble, remove, throw in the woods off trail, replace and repeat. See how easy life can be at only $29.95 for three. I hear the profits trickling in now.

Next, Ken's Denture Straps (applied only by certified dentists.) A three-inch monofilament line, coiled under a lower rear molar, attached by a tiny screw inserted into the jawbone. Nothing is worse than standing on top of the waterfalls along the Falling Waters Trail as your 83-year-old squeeze standing below with camera yells "Smile." As you obey the command, a black fly goes into your mouth causing you to cough, expelling your dentures while you watch them go flying down the 80-foot waterfall, leaving you toothless and, even worse, without that great picture. No worries, with my new Ken's Denture Straps what would have been a disaster is simply hanging three inches out of your mouth. Go ahead, Pops, and pop them back in, get that picture and later recoil the line. Don't be like the guy who goes to spit off Rogers Ledge and loses those pearly whites. Get Ken's Denture Straps for $250 with installation, not including dentures.

Let's not forget about hearing aids. "What?" So juvenile. Haha. Batteries on hearing aids are small and can die out quickly. No one wants to miss the lifesaving warning of "Wet rocks!" The next thing you know you have fallen and broken a hip, fo' shame! That need never happen with Ken's Solar Powered Hearing Aids. A simple, almost invisible wire connecting your hearing aid to a small solar panel on the top of your "I Hiked with Ken" hat does the trick. You do not have to miss the sounds of nature or the flatulence of your hiking companions ever again. Only $24.29. I hear the phone ringing and it's Forbes magazine.

You say your pace has diminished in the last year? You do not have to be the slow poke any longer. Get Ken's Speed Up Your Pace kit. This simple, yet proven, pace-acceleration kit contains Ex-Lax and pepper. The easy-to-follow instructions will advise you to take three Ex-Lax tablets the morning of your hike up Mount Isolation. When you notice your pace dropping off, you apply pepper to your upper lip. The irresistible urge to sneeze with the now unstoppable pressure of rectal drainage will have you moving like a 20-year-old. The kit costs $19.55. In case of mishaps, be sure to stock up on Ken's Camo Colored Biodegradable Hiking Depends. Caution: sometimes the brute force of a colon blowout can be so powerful as to cause you to dislodge your dentures with such force the monofilament line can break. Make sure to carry the replacement lines at $9.45. Also advised is to pick up extra "I Hiked with Ken" hat solar panels for the low price of $8.29.

Mild brain fog can easily lead to accidentally wandering off trail. Keith comes to mind for the application of Ken's Brain Fog AllTrails Shock Collar. Say Keith is pushing 100 and he is acting very strange. He cannot follow a conversation, drools a lot, has a neck and head twitch, and is constantly blowing his nose into his hand. In that case he is acting normally, but let's say things get really weird. The poor guy is always wandering off trail, mumbling something about mowing lawns and camping out on wheels. No worries, the collar does all the work for you. Powerful GPS signals, aligned with AllTrails mapping system and a nine-volt battery collar, will automatically detect a three-foot variation off trail and gently shock the opposite side of his neck causing him to drift back onto the trail. There may be slight yelping or deep grunting sounds with each mild shock, but it is worth it knowing your aged hiker will stay on track. Make sure to read the instructions carefully as too high a setting can have the same effect as Ken's Speed Up Your Pace kit. Confer with your PCP before use. Your safety is our main concern even while our profits will be shocking at $235.29 per customer.

Of course, for someone still in the prime of their 80's, like Ian, we will also offer Ken's Black Diamond Flex Z Walkers, Oboz Orthopedic Hikers and Quad-Focal Eyeglasses that allow toe-to-trail vision. Also, custom made for Ian will be Ken's Oh Crap, Look at That Steep Section Pacemaker. This will instantly allow for a runaway heart to be shocked into a normal rhythm. However, like Ken's Speed Up Your Pace Kit or Ken's Brain Farts AllTrails Shock Collar, the shocking effect will call for an ample supply of Camo Colored Biodegradable Hiking Depends. On the bright side, they make excellent Christmas gifts.

Contact me if you are interested in stock options.

36   THE HIKER BABES

There is a lady — for privacy purposes, I will call Katie (her real name is Katie) — whom I befriended on Facebook after seeing her zeal in talking to others about my books. She is an avid hiker and her posts revealed she did a lot of hiking with a New Hampshire group called Hiker Babes.

Me being me and always looking for a good hiking story, I reached out to Katie and inquired about the possibility of a hike with The Hiker Babes. Truth is stranger than fiction and, though somewhat repressed by PTSD, the story you are about to read is my account of the day I hiked with the Hiker Babes.

Foul weather should have been my first clue as Katie and I made plans for the hike. She told me a number of ladies were excited about the hike that would take place on a Wednesday, and she was targeting the two-summit hike over Welch-Dickey. The forecast was calling for rain from Monday through Tuesday night. In Ken McGray's "52 With A View: A Hiker's Guide," there is a warning that states "The steep slab rock on Welch-Dickey is slippery when wet." Being an experienced hiker and a little bit of a chicken, I voiced strong objections about hiking those peaks. I recommended we wait for a dryer day. Katie, being a woman, countered with a guilt trip, that a few of the women had already taken the day off work. (Kudos to Johnny Depp, the only man to win an argument with a woman!) While still dazed by Katie's negotiations skills, I signed off on Mount Monadnock. It is higher and, in some areas, steeper than Welch-Dickey. Yay me!

Not knowing Katie super well, I was shocked to see a car with Massachusetts plates pull into my driveway. As I got in, I was humming the tune, "When the Rolls Are Called Up Yonder, I'll Be There." The drive to pick up two other ladies was exactly what I imagined, white knuckles and all, and I may have broken the O.S.

handle in her car. She apologized for her lack of night vision. Remove "night" from her statement. Her GPS was a Garmin unit made in the 1980's. It was programed for the "See the country" setting, as it took us in a figure-eight pattern across southern New Hampshire.

Just when I thought the worst was over, we loaded up the other two ladies. Marie was sweet and quiet, while Melissa was funny and could cuss like a cross between a U.S. Marine and a Canadian lumberjack. It did not phase me as my mom was French and taught me how to swear in two languages. Melissa is also one of the ambassadors for the Hiker Babes. Once again Katie's GPS, pulled from the original Mercury Space Craft, had us on dirt roads. I never remembered dirt roads on my trips to Monadnock, yet there we were. We were now 45 minutes late and Melissa had to pee, so Katie pulled over, I looked out my window and saw a stone wall with nice woods and large trees just beyond, offering the perfect outdoors facilities. A few seconds later, I happened to glance in the passenger mirror and there was Melissa squatting by the side of the car letting it rip. I am legally blind in one eye, but just then my good eye misted over, and I went brain blind. I thought Holy Cow!!! She must know Dave! What had I gotten myself into?

Back on the road with my vision slowly returning, we arrived at the parking lot, and I was introduced to the other six ladies. We packed up and headed out. The woods were still dripping wet from the night of rain and Stacy (a delightful gal who is an ambassador for Hiker Babes) said, "If the rocks are wet, I am turning around." Right then she became my best friend. I do not like wet rocks. I had already fallen on Monadnock from wet rock and had recently fallen on Paugus from wet rock and sprained my left wrist. We headed up the White Dot trail. At the junction of Cascade Link was the first photo-op. This is when I began to discover that the Hiker Babes stop at every sign, river, rock formation, flower and moss-covered tree to take pictures. It is not that they take pictures of things as much as they take pictures of themselves with things in the background. At times they will even take individual pictures so that all 10 of them paraded into position, one after the other, and get that perfect pic. I thought Dave and Ian were bad; these gals take pictures by the hundreds.

By this time, we were navigating wet, slippery rocks. Between the two prior days of rain and the relentless humidity, the condition of the rocks was getting worse. I kept glancing over at Stacy, wondering when she would put an end to the madness. Dang, she pushed on like a trooper. We arrived at the Spellman Trail. On the map it is marked by tiny dots, with a footnote saying "Footpath — may be more challenging." What?!? Megan stepped up and said, "I'll lead the way." I believe Megan secretly belongs to a woman's branch of the Navy Seals. She is also an ambassador for Hiking Babes. She had just hiked Mount Saint Helens and was now guiding us up Mount Hell. Spellman has to be a Terrifying 25 entry! (It isn't.) Megan pushed on and Stacy refused to give me an out. I was stuck going up some crazy rock scrambles. All the ladies were amazing hikers. At one overview, Megan stopped, so I passed her and scrambled up a little higher. As she was catching up to me, I came face to face with a two-foot snake sunning itself on the trail. We startled each other and it slithered under a rock. I announced its presence and found Megan is not a fan of snakes. As a matter of fact, she somehow teleported from 10 feet behind me to 20 feet in front of me. I never saw anything like that. From here to there ... boom! As I was questioning their choice of trails, I discovered it was none other than Katie who chose this route because there was a secret, surprise location she wanted to see that included a quarter-mile one-way bushwhack. I had already unfollowed her on Facebook and was now unfriending her. After locating the mysterious destination, we stopped for lunch. It was only 10 a.m. These gals were breaking out sandwiches, salads, cheeseburgers ... I have got to start hiking more often with these ladies. They know how to pack a lunch. I settled in with my Cliff bar that soon lost all its appeal in the presence of the buffet I was surrounded by. Their nurturing side came out after they saw me crying and they all offered me food, yet I could hear Keith's voice in my head saying, "You are shameless," so I declined their kind offers.

As we were hiking, I kept feeling lightheaded and I did not know why until it dawned on me that these 10 ladies talked so much they sucked the oxygen out of a 30-foot radius around them. They talked about the hike, their gear, fashion, work, Covid, the weather, their kids, their husbands (I took notes, guys, and for a small fee I will gladly share) — they talked about everything non-stop. I am usually a talker, too, but I am kind of shy around new people, so I quietly listened as my ears slowly melted off my head. I got to know Karen who is a fellow Christian and super-nice lady. She had strained her back, so Megan was carrying her supplies as well as her own. Nice move, Karen. I will have to see if I can use that on Dave. Just kidding. By the end of the hike she was in some discomfort and I felt bad for her. Patty, I discovered, is the photo bomb queen. I would sense a presence on my side and, poof, just like that she had a picture of the two of us. When she struck up her famous bow-and-arrow pose, I could not help but sneak up behind her with my hand as a visor over my eyes, looking like her guide, peering at her faraway target.

There was a consensus among the group that we would skip the summit as it was socked in, and everyone had been there multiple times. Usually, I push on and summit no matter what, but I had an appointment that evening and was concerned Katie's GPS may route us through New York, so I agreed, and we started down. We took the Pumpelly Trial north to the Cascade Trail heading south, which would eventually connect us back with the White Dot Trail that we had taken going up. There were plenty of stops for photos. Dear Lord, photos!

We stopped to see an Imp Face-like bolder formation. The girls were in photo heaven. I did not take a picture as it looked exactly like Ian, and I see him all the time. I took off and got ahead of the tribe when I heard someone say, "Look, Ken has finally had enough of us witches." (Not the exact word used.) I offered for someone else to lead and Megan took off like a rocket. I was again in the lead for the rest of the group, when I came upon a nasty section of slab rock, worn smooth and covered in a thin layer of wet slime. I headed off to the right with two ladies following. Katie was next, but she was far enough back to have not seen the way we went. We then heard a terrifying scream, so I yelled back "Stay right!" Katie had almost fallen, but she used cat-like reflexes and then yelled back "Oh thanks, Ken, you're a doll." I was flattered so much that within a short distance we came upon a repeat of the wet, moss-covered rock and this time I yelled back, "Katie, stay right!" I do what I can to help. There is a famous story about a little girl named Sarah Witcher who at three years old got lost in these parts for four days. When they found her, she was with a black bear who had kept her warm and alive. I could tell from

Katie's voice if she were the bear and I was a lost little boy . . . I wouldn't have stood a chance. Hahaha. What a crew.

Here is where the story takes a turn into what I felt was the most amazing thing I had ever witnessed. It would have been equal to seeing Bigfoot, riding on the Loch Ness Monster, shooting a Lazar gun at attacking UFOs. Amy, who has lightning-quick sarcasm was going slow on the way down. Alicia, who has an award-winning smile, was staying with her, so I figured I would hang back with them to make sure everything was OK. They got into a conversation ... for 25 minutes ... that had no break in it. I mean NONE! Amy would talk for a full minute and, somehow using telepathy, Alicia would know when she was done and, within a millisecond, start the next sentence. Back and forth they went non-stop for 25 minutes. Every now and then I thought I would throw my two cents into the ring but nothing doing. They never gave me the chance. How in the world did they do it? I have never experienced anything like it. If I had not been stupefied, I would have recorded it. But it was hypnotic. I know neurologists say most brain functions of women pass through the speech center of the brain, but this was ALL speech center. They didn't just talk, they verbally danced. They flowed in and out of topics never losing a beat. Ladies, I tip my hat to you. That was quite a performance.

The next thing I knew we were back at the parking lot where book signings and more photos abounded. Monique, who is as sweet as apple pie, made sure I spelled her name with the "que" at the end, explaining it was French. I liked her even more. We all said our goodbyes and headed out ... for ice cream. I did not see that coming. I learned it is a ritual with these gals. Katie was nice enough to buy me a chocolate shake even though I did not warn her about the slippery rocks. That is the way these girls roll. Had it been the goons I hiked with I would have had to pay for all of them.

In the car Katie, Melissa and Marie were talking about their annual Halloween hike up Middle Sugarloaf in full costume. Knowing how Dave feels about costumes, I recommended he hike with them. Katie shot back "As long as he wears a Tutu." Ha, that would be a sight. I later got thinking about it and thought what a Halloween hike would be like with my goons and the Hiker Babes? Good God, that would be something.

On the way home, Katie's GPS steered us off the direct route of Interstate 93 and led us right through the city of Manchester for no good reason. It did not even bother me for I was content with the events of the day.

All in all, it was a great hike and I had a blast. Thanks so much, Hiker Babes!

Hiker Babes is a national organization with chapters all over the country. Each chapter has a four-point rating system that allows potential newcomers to know what kind of group they are hiking with. Here is the rating:

1) Kind, considerate, friendly and fun

2) Kind, friendly

3) Friendly, somewhat crazy

4) Crazy

I'll never forget my hike with Group 5.

37 When Hell Freezes Over

Where to begin?

After hiking with the Hiker Babes, I noticed discomfort in my right foot. Turns out I had developed inflammation in my Achilles tendon, causing considerable discomfort to walk, let alone hike. Those women broke me! They are one tough bunch. Way tougher than the goons.

I had taken 3 weeks off to rest when Dave got the idea for an overnighter. He roped Ian in and the next thing I knew they were harassing me to join them. "Only if it is a flat hike," I countered. My ankle was still tender and I did not want to have a setback. They found a flat hike to a pond and I agreed to go.

The weather was to be clear, no wind but a bit chilly in the high 30's. Since this was Columbus Day weekend, I figured it may be the last overnighter of the year, yet I was a little concerned about crowds. The guys assured me no one would be spending a night at an obscure pond.

Dave showed up at 2:20 p.m. and we left to meet Ian in Concord. Ian had a NH Park sticker on his vehicle so we loaded into his car. We stopped at a Subway and got our dinner, and during the drive up the conversation turned to all the great overnighters we had spent on mountains. The next thing I knew we were headed for Mount Willard with 900 feet of elevation gain. I did not want to be a buzz kill so I silently hoped my ankle would handle a mild mountain hike.

The traffic was heavy, and all out of state. People love to visit NH for the foliage, which was at peak. By the time we hit Franconia Notch traffic was bumper to bumper and barely moving. I am always loving and accommodating to others, but Dave and Ian were starting to get sour attitudes. Arriving at the parking lot they went from sour to ticked at the lack of parking. We found a spot, geared up, and headed up. There must have been 200 hundred people streaming down. Unfortunately, not being from the US, let alone NH, they did not comprehend trail etiquette and refused to allow ascending hikers the right of way. By now Dave and Ian were sputtering and spitting like a cat with a hairball. I reminded them to be kind because you reap what you sow. They quieted down a bit.

Half the trail was wet with water running down it. We still made good time, and my foot did surprisingly well. At the summit I had to listen to their rumblings over a guy illegally flying a drone, and another group playing loud music through a boom-box. I reminded them to just let it go. We ate our supper and located a place in the woods to bed down. A full moon crested the silhouetted range of Mount Webster, while a foreboding chill forced the temps down. I sensed a grim reaping of the bad attitudes.

Ian lied to me about a 40% chance of rain coming in early morning, while Dave started playing Lord Huron music after complaining about the people who had boomboxes. Then they both started in on me as they witnessed me unpack my favorite blue blanket I had brought for extra warmth. It occurred to me their reaping was imminent. In my innocence I prayed I would not be included with guilt by association. I moved my sleeping bag ten feet away from theirs to be clear of the lightning bolt blast zone.

Temperatures plummeted so we all retreated to the warmth of our sleeping bags by 6:45 p.m. It would be a long night, as sunrise was not till 6:45 a.m. I had a zero-degree rated bag with my blanket, two down jackets, a thick winter hat and my winter mitts. Dave was in shorts with a moderate sleeping bag and bag liner, while Ian had a moderate bag and quilt. My sleep was interrupted by the most awful racket one could imagine. They were both snoring like a couple of bears dying of COPD. On top of that, they were freezing, and their chattering teeth sounded like machine gun fire: a growl, followed by a rata-tat-tat. I almost felt bad for them as I was so toasty warm that had I removed my blanket to use as an extra thick pillow. I listened for a while longer as they constantly tossed and turned. It was sad. I soon drifted off to peaceful rest, yet sometime later awakened by alarmed voices and lights flashing this way and that way. I was semi-conscious, so never did find out what was going on. Once again in the early morning hours I was roused by a ruckus to find Dave's new Nemo air pad had deflated. No matter how many times he blew it up, it would go flat again, leaving him no other option than trying to sleep on the hard, cold, frozen, forest floor.

I awoke to relieve myself around 4 a.m. only to hear the familiar growl, and rata-tat-tat. I was really starting to feel sorry for the two. They are not bad guys, just sometimes misguided, I feel that is why I am in their lives, so I can give direction.

With our morning coffee, the night's episode came tumbling out. Dave had awakened in the night and came face to face with a baby porcupine. The unamused creature grunted an obscenity at him then scurried off to a nearby tree. Dave's mild scream had awakened Ian, as well as every animal within 5,000 feet. Ian and Dave then resorted to using their headlamps like anti-aircraft gunners looking for an invading force, terrifying the little, quilled, mammal who in turn, launched a barbed projectile into Dave's Nemo.

Dave and Ian looked like they had been on a 10-day binger. Their puffy faces, swollen eyes, and disheveled looks were matched by their voices that sounded like hell, which by the way HAD frozen over, as the temps dropped into the 20's with gusting winds that had arisen in the night, along with the porcupine.

Well, like they say, "Karma's a b... not a nice person."

I think I am going to take up hiking with the Hiker Babes. It is a lot easier with less drama.

38 Last Overnighter of the Season

The weather warmed, the forecast turned favorable, the goons went goofy. It is always the same, on Monday morning they view the 10-day forecast. Seeing a nice Friday night, they start the "Who's in for an overnighter?" By Wednesday they are going mental because I have not responded. It never ceases to amaze me, after hiking 8 years in the most inconsistent weather in the country, that they expect an extended forecast to hold. By Thursday they were ready to do bodily harm, and demanded, "Are you going or NOT!" Being totally shocked that the weather actually remained unchanged, I responded, "Of course, why wouldn't I?"

This is how an overnighter usually goes in our crew; I had found a small, spray can of fart bomb. I had discharged some in my car after Dave had gotten in on our last trip. After almost puking from the foul, putrid odor, Dave insisted we get Ian with it on our next trip. This was that trip. We met at EMS in Concord. Ian sat in the front. As Dave got in the back seat, I slipped him the can. A few minutes later, Dave nonchalantly asked how everyone's week had gone. I commented that I felt a little queasy. A short time later, I locked the windows and Dave let it rip. In seconds we were all gasping, yet Dave and I were crying in hysterics as Ian had one hand over his nose and the other on the door handle while screaming, "If you don't unlock the #*&$(#\ windows I am opening this door!" Seeing I was doing 80 mph I decided to unlock the windows. Ian was not impressed by our antics. The next few miles we froze our buns off as we drove with the windows down trying to eliminate the horrible smell.

Stopping at Subway I told the goons I did not want anything. I was not hungry. They got their sandwiches and we drove to the trailhead. We put on our packs and headed up to spend the night on some ledges. Sometime before this Ian had bought two bear bells that we could wear to drive Dave nuts. Ian had forgotten his but I brought mine. It was all chuckles at first, but after 1.7 miles Dave was pretty annoyed. To be truthful, I think we were all getting tired of the clatter. When I finally put the bell away, Dave insisted it never go on another hike. Someone was getting testy. Hehehe.

We put out our sleep systems, then sat on the ledges for supper. It was getting cold, so you can imagine their surprise as I produced a thermos of steaming hot soup and a ham and cheese sandwich with Dorito's. They turned green with envy as they sullenly chomped on their cold subs. I may have rubbed it in a little with some satisfied grunts and yummy groans. I knew if I pushed it too much, they would throw me off the ledges just to get my tomato and cauliflower soup. Did they get even? Would they be that immature? Oh ya! It was not until I was home and unpacked that I found all their trash in the bottom of my pack. To make matters worse, my pack was soaked with beer and Italian dressing. (It's not like that could attract bears or anything. JERKS!)

We spent a cool, yet enjoyable night out. It was in the mid-thirties, no wind, and a star filled sky. We were in our sleeping bags by 7:45 p.m. and sunrise was at 7 a.m. That is a long time to lay around. I slept for a few hours, then would watch the sky for shooting stars or satellites. I counted about 20 satellites during the course of the night. I did end up getting around 7 hours of sleep and awoke refreshed.

We took pics of an epic sunrise while we heated up our morning coffee. We lingered for a time, then decided to head out as we heard voices approaching. On the way down, Ian stopped to de-layer. While he and Dave were distracted, I slipped away and started my semi-run down the mountain just so I could move the car in the parking lot and watch them search for it in their usual confused, disoriented, brain-dead, way.

It is all about having a fun experience. Darlene is always amazed that we continue hiking together, let alone talk with each other. You need to choose your hiking buddies carefully. You want to find fun, kind, giving, likeable people, or you will end up with goons like those I hike with.

39 Conclusion

I hope you have found this book entertaining. I love making people laugh. These books have been an unexpected, yet delightful, journey for me. I want to thank you for following along with me. Whether you are a hiker or not, I pray you get out and enjoy nature. I love the beauty of mountains, the feeling of being in a deep forest, blue sky and sunshine.

For me, the belief in evolution takes too much faith. I simply cannot believe that everything came from nothing. There is too much design. This planet orbits the sun on what scientists call the knife edge. A little closer, we would burn. A little farther, we would freeze. We have just the right amount of atmosphere, water and soil. Earth was designed to inhabit life. Look outward at the billions of galaxies that take hundreds of millions of light years to traverse. Look inward at the complexity of code in DNA.

When you look at your cell phone you know that the technology and design did not just happen, yet how much more complex is the human mind that designed the phone? Where there is design, there is a designer.

In the Bible, the Book of Romans, Chapter 1, Verse 20 says, "For since the creation of the world, His invisible attributes, His eternal power and divine nature, have been clearly seen, being understood through what has been made,"

Life is a gift. Where there is a gift, there is a gift giver. What if you could actually come to know this God who created all things? What if He revealed Himself? What if He loved you so much, He invited you to know Him? The good news is … He has. If you dare, let me show you how.

I am blown away by the number of hikers who want to meet me just because I have written a few books. Maybe it is because in those books I reveal that I am a nutcase and people can relate to my flawed humanity. What if God became one of us to reveal who He really is? What if it was written in a book, unlike any other book, and He would actually reveal Himself and speak to you through that book?

I challenge you to an experiment.

Get a copy of the Gospel of John. With an open mind, pray "God, if you are real, would you reveal yourself to me and speak to me?" Then read just a few paragraphs and ask these simple questions as you reread the text:

1) What does this reveal to me about people or humanity in general?

2) What does this reveal to me about God or Jesus?

3) What does God want to say to me personally?

I promise you that if you go through the Gospels in sincerity, things will happen. Nature is cool, but the God of nature is way cooler.

Enjoy the hike.

About The Editor

Mike Trocchi lives in East Haddam, Conn., and is a longtime journalist and editor. He is the former sports editor at two daily newspapers, one of which (Foster's Daily Democrat in Dover, N.H.) for years published noted White Mountains author Mike Dickerman's weekly hiking column "Along the Beaten Path." He has also worked as copy editor and digital editor for Active Interest Media and is currently employed at a defense contractor.

Trocchi's love of hiking in the Whites has spurred him to climb all 48 of New Hampshire's 4,000 footers, dozens more than once. He is currently working on several other hiking lists, including the 52 With A View, the Terrifying 25, the New England Hundred Highest and, most importantly, the Winter 48.

He'd like to thank Dickerman and AMC White Mountain Guide editor Steve Smith for their support, guidance and insight through the years. Both gentlemen are this generation's treasures and sages for those who wish to climb these mountains for years to come.

He'd also like to thank longtime hiking partners Harrison Haas, David Cowan, Steve Barbour, Scott Bruns, Ashley Smith, Jean Bagnati, Suzzy Deets and Corey Stanchina for their many hours of enjoyment on the trails. He'd especially like to thank his father, from whom the desire to tramp about in the woods for hours, searching and seeing, wandering and wondering, came about.

His only compensation for editing this book was a copy of Ken's second and third books. His refund request for the first one is still pending at press time.

Mike can be reached at mikejtrocchi@gmail.com

About the Author

Ken and his wife Darlene reside in Raymond, NH, where he has served as pastor of a local church for over 30 years. Their daughter and son-in-law live in NH and have two young children while their son and daughter-in-law, who live in the Nevada High Sierras, have a daughter and twin boys on the way. They all enjoy the outdoors.

Ken is the Chaplain at the Raymond Police Department. He is also a PCC Level Life Coach with the International Coaching Federation. He has trained and coached individuals, couples and workplace teams, helping them to achieve their goals in life.

He enjoys riding motorcycles, photography, playing guitar, shooting, cycling, kayaking with Darlene and writing.

Other Books by This Author

Available through
Bondcliff Books, Littleton, NH
Mountain Wanderer, Lincoln, NH
Amazon

THEY SAID IT WOULD BE FUN

A Hilarious Journey Learning to Hike the NH 48

What doesn't kill you makes you stronger . . . or so they say . . . unless you are old and out of shape while attempting to take up hiking. Ken takes you on humorous adventures in the NH White Mountains as he tackles the NH 48 4,000 footers. Young or old, experienced hiker or beginner, you will get lots of laughs learning the finer lessons of hiking.

Profits from book sales will go to New Hampshire Search and Rescue.

THEY SAID THEY WANTED MORE

A Hilarious Journey Hiking the NH 52 With a View

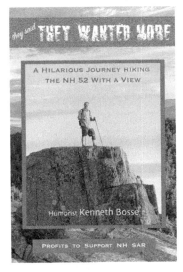

People have called Ken not right in the head, funny, whacky, crazy and hilarious. He really doesn't care as long as they call him to hike.

Once again Ken uses his satirical warped sense of humor, making light of the struggles of hiking the "52 With a View" while incessantly menacing his friends. This time he has mixed it up by adding hiking tips and having contributors tell some tales.

New Hampshire is a hiker's paradise. However, each year many are injured, and sadly some die. Hikers need to be prepared. NH is home to some of the bravest and best trained SAR volunteers. These men and women venture out in some of the worst conditions on the planet and it is relief to know if you get into trouble, help is on the way.

If you are not a hiker, enjoy this peek into the world of hiking and then run for the hills.

As with his first book, profits go to NH SAR. For that we say thank you for your purchase.

Made in the USA
Middletown, DE
26 September 2023

39277016R00106